JAPANESE COUNCIL
INSTITUTE OF PACIFIC RELATIONS

"FAR EASTERN CONFLICT" SERIES

FOREIGN POLICY OF JAPAN:

1914 – 1939

FOREIGN POLICY OF JAPAN:
1914–1939

By

MASAMICHI RŌYAMA

"FAR EASTERN CONFLICT" SERIES

GREENWOOD PRESS, PUBLISHERS
WESTPORT, CONNECTICUT

Library of Congress Cataloging in Publication Data

Rōyama, Masamichi, 1895-
　　Foreign policy of Japan:　1914-1939.

　　Reprint of the 1941 ed. published by the
Japanese Council, Institute of Pacific Relations,
Tokyo, which was issued as no. 7 of "Far Eastern
conflict" series.
　　Bibliography:　p.
　　1.　Japan--Foreign relations--1912-1945.
2.　Eastern question (Far East)　I.　Title.
II.　Series:　"Far Eastern conflict" series, no. 7.
DS885.R68　1973　　　327.52　　　　73-3930
ISBN　0-8371-6853-8

Originally published in 1941
by the Japanese Council, Institute of Pacific Relations, Tokyo

First Greenwood Reprinting 1973

Library of Congress Catalogue Card Number 73-3930

ISBN 0-8371-6853-8

Printed in the United States of America

FOREWORD

The conflict which is in progress in the Far East is undoubtedly one of the most epochal events in the history of the Eastern hemisphere. Whatever may have been its immediate occasion, its ultimate issue now is likely to produce profound effects upon both struggling nations, upon the other foreign powers concerned, and upon the international relations in China as a whole. It will be, indeed, in this last respect that the most important feature of the conflict is to be found. Considering the fact that these relations have not only been extraordinarily complex, but also involve vital national interests, both economic and political, one can easily appreciate the intensity of the struggle and the repercussions which any transformation in the Far Eastern situation would precipitate. If it is too much to say that the outbreak of the conflict was inevitable in the light of the international relations then existing in this area, at least one can believe that the conflict was destined from the very first to give rise to issues which were world-wide. Moreover, with the combat of political ideologies threatening to occupy the foreground of strife throughout the world, one cannot foretell how much farther the gravity of the situation will be intensified. One is certain, however, that the outcome of the conflict will have a decisive bearing upon the peace and well-being of all the peoples on earth for years to come.

The present volume constitutes part of the series of studies organized by the Japanese Council, Institute of Pacific Relations, upon some facts and problems relevant to this conflict in the Far East. As will be clear from the Editor's Preface, the series deals only with those subjects which are directly related to the economic and political conditions of Japan and her foreign policy. It is also admittedly a survey essentially pursued from the Japanese point of view. It is hoped, however, that the fact that it presents national views and problems will prove to make the studies particularly valuable, provided, of course, that it does so with a scholarly spirit worthy of the I.P.R. Lastly it represents an effort to provide accurate knowledge of the conflict which may serve as basis of a just and durable peace, although it does not presume to suggest any specific plan for settlement whatever. If it contributes to the understanding of the part played by Japan in the conflict, or if it throws any light upon the peculiarities and complexities of the Far Eastern situation, the Japanese Council will have been fully rewarded.

Mention must be made of the Inquiry Series organized by the Institute of Pacific Relations into problems arising from the conflict. As a matter of fact, the publication of the present series is, in a sense, an outcome of the initiative taken by that body, but the Japanese Council has found it unable to participate in that particular undertaking. For the organization and publication of its own series, the Japanese Council alone is responsible.

Tadao Yamakawa

Vice-Chairman
Japanese Council
Institute of Pacific Relations

April 4, 1941

EDITOR'S PREFACE

The "Far Eastern Conflict" series published by the Japanese Council of the Institute of Pacific Relations consists of the following seven volumes :

I. Introductory Studies on the Sino-Japanese Conflict, by K. Miki and K. Hosokawa ;
II. Recent Political and Economic Developments in Japan, by H. Sassa and S. Ryū ;
III. Recent Political and Economic Developments in Manchoukuo, by Y. Koizumi ;
IV. Problems in the Occupied Areas in China, by T. Itō ;
V. An Analysis of Japanese Foreign Policy since the Restoration, by S. Yabe ;
VI. Sino-Japanese Relations in the Twentieth Century, by H. Ozaki ;
VII. Foreign Policy of Japan : 1914–1939, by M. Rōyama.

The Introductory Studies (Vol. I) consist of two separate surveys which form a historical approach to the present conflict in the Far East—namely, (1) A History of the Sino-Japanese Cultural Relations, Prior to the Advent of the Western Powers, and (2) The Advance of the Western Powers and Its Impact on the East.

The Recent Political and Economic Developments in Japan (Vol. II) also comprises two different studies by different authors :— (1) The Development and Trends of Japanese Politics, by Mr. Hirō Sassa, and (2) The Recent Economic Development in Japan, by Mr. Shintarō Ryū. The close relationship between internal and international policies has increasingly come to be realized by scholars in different countries. The first essay is a brief survey of the political and social development in modern Japan ; the second deals with its economic and financial development ; and both of them are presented with the hope of furnishing the requisite knowledge on domestic situations as a basis for understanding present international affairs.

The next two studies on Manchoukuo (Vol. III) and on the so-called Occupied Areas in China (Vol. IV) undertake an accurate account of the conditions and problems in these countries. No one

can reasonably expect to attain a real understanding of the Far
Eastern controversy without balanced information bearing on this
phase of the situation.

The last three studies deal with Japanese foreign policy. Professor Yabe's brief survey is an attempt to furnish a general historical approach to the study of international relations leading up to
the present conflict (Vol. V). Mr. Ozaki deals specifically with
Recent Sino-Japanese Relations (Vol. VI). And Professor Rōyama
undertakes to expound the New Order in East Asia, together with
his own analysis of Japan's Recent Far Eastern Policy (Vol. VII).

The present volume, which is the last of the series on the Far
Eastern Conflict, consists of two parts, written by Mr. Masamichi
Rōyama, formerly professor of political science at the Tokyo Imperial
University, sometime lecturer on Japanese History and Politics at
the University of Hawaii, director of Tokyo Institute of Political and
Economic Research and author of several books, including " Principles of the Science of Administration " (1928), "Studies on Relations
between Japan and Manchuria " (1933), and " Contemporary Political
History of Japan " (1940). In Part I the author undertakes to present
his views and interpretations of the main currents in the foreign policy
of Japan since the World War of 1914–1918, and brings his account
down to the Manchurian Incident. In Part II he inquires both into
the development and nature of Japanese policy which culminated in
the proclamation of the establishment of a New Order in East Asia
as the ultimate objective of the conflict, and into certain major
problems which necessarily arose in Japan's relations with China and
other powers as a result of that same policy.

In tracing the historical background of the Sino-Japanese Conflict,
with emphasis upon the period after the Manchurian Incident, the
author explains how in 1935 both China and Japan were striving
for conciliation and cooperation, even at the risk of arousing violent
political passions at home ; wherein lay the insurmountable obstacle ;
how the fateful moment descended to the two peoples ; and how finally in the autumn of 1938, out of the somewhat confused, undefined
principles which had guided Japanese policy up till that time, emerged
the conception of a New Order in East Asia—a conception which
embodies Japan's full recognition of rising nationalism in China and
her deep realization that a close and reciprocal association between
the two nations is the keynote of a new order of things in the

Orient.

No Japanese is sanguine enough to claim that the New Order exists already in full swing. On the contrary every true Japanese realizes that the actual state of things falls far short of the ideal. And the author points out that, legalistically, the New Order as envisaged by Japan cannot be considered established until it is formally recognized internationally, and that the hostile attitude of many foreign powers at present is mainly caused by the confusion on their part of taking the existing state of affairs as the New Order itself.

The most important point in connection with this new policy, as the author asserts, lies in the fact that it is based upon the fundamental conviction of Japan that the proposed New Order, and the proposed New Order alone, will offer the real solution for the age-long problem : independent, strong and prosperous China. Underneath seemingly contradictory phenomena of various kinds, here is a truly constructive effort to lay the foundation for a new Asia and thus a new world; here is a challenge claiming the most serious attention of every citizen of the world.

Part I was a separate study originally started as a contribution to the international research program of the I.P.R., but with the consent of that institution, has been included in the present volume. The uniformity in writing may, therefore, be slightly lacking, but the advantage should be obvious.

It should be also remarked that Part II was written in the autumn of 1939, and therefore does not include in its discussion the momentous events since then, which necessarily had their world-wide repercussions.

For the translation of this volume into English Mr. Tomohiko Ushiba is primarily responsible.

For the pursuance of the work of this " Far Eastern Conflict " series, a board of editors has been appointed which consists of several members, including Messrs. Tomohiko Ushiba, Kinkazu Saionji, Samitarō Uramatsu and Shigeharu Matsumoto. This board is primarily responsible for the general organization and conduct of the whole series. For the statements of facts and views appearing in the several volumes, however, the respective authors are solely responsible.

The board of editors is greatly indebted to a number of authorities and especially the authors of the series, to whom every one of draft copies of the studies has been submitted, and who have cooperated generously with their criticisms and suggestions. It feels grateful also to several foreign friends for their valuable help and suggestions in matters relating to translation of the Series ; and especially to Dr. Brooks Emeny, Mr. Philip E. Lilienthal and Dr. E. Herbert Norman in connection with this volume. It is indebted to Miss H. Matsukata and Miss Y. Matsuoka for their kind help in reading the proofs.

Although every member of the small staff of the Japanese Council has contributed to the editorial work of this series, special acknowledgment is due to Mr. Kōhei Yagawa, Miss Hanako Iwanaga and Mr. Genji Ōkubo, who have carried the major burden of the tremendous amount of details attendant upon this kind of work of translation and publication, a matter scarcely appreciated outside of Japan.

Yasaka Takagi
Chairman
Board of Editors

Tokyo
July 7, 1941

CONTENTS

INTRODUCTION

A GENERAL SURVEY OF JAPAN'S
FOREIGN POLICY

INTRODUCTION

A GENERAL SURVEY OF JAPAN'S
FOREIGN POLICY

Japan's diplomatic relations with foreign countries in modern times began with the Meiji era, after her emergence from the rigorously self-imposed seclusion of 260 years under the feudalistic Tokugawa regime. Her foreign policy at that time was directed to the attainment of national security and equality with other members of the family of nations. The political situation of the world in general and of the Far East in particular was so turbulent owing to the growth of aggressive nationalism that it was natural for this forcibly opened and weak nation to devote her utmost energy to develop her military and industrial strength in order to secure her position as an independent state free from encroachments by Western powers.

Japan's diplomatic activities were pursued in two directions. One was towards her two Asiatic neighbours, China and Korea, with a view to securing their recognition of the new position which she had acquired through the Restoration. Thus, when the internal disorders of several years had been settled and her consolidation as a modern state had progressed, negotiations were undertaken to secure the recognition of her new status by these countries. The other direction concerned the Western powers, the object here being to abolish the "unequal" treaties to which Japan had been subjected since the establishment of regular diplomatic intercourse with these countries. It was obvious that these treaties were not only detrimental to her economic development, but that they constituted a serious obstacle to her aspiration of attaining national equality with the advanced nations of the world.

The achievement of these two diplomatic aims was inter-dependent in the sense that the success of one direction was the necessary precondition for the success of the other. For as long as the Western powers would not recognize the en-hanced position of Japan among the Asiatic nations, the latter would not acknowledge the great change in Japan's political order, nor its significant bearing upon international relations in the Far East. On the other hand, unless the Asiatic nations themselves granted it, the Western powers would not concede a privileged position to Japan, but would treat the Far East as a whole as a half-civilized or semi-colonial area since they were ignorant of the uniqueness of the history and character-istics of the Japanese.

Accordingly, Japan was doubly determined to become powerful in the military sense and civilized by Western standards. As the situation in the Far East developed, Japan had to fight first with China and then with Russia over the problem of Korea. And it was through these two adventures that she at last accomplished her aim, for they demonstrated unmistakably to the outside world that for the first time in her history she had established herself as a great power on the Asiatic continent, and that she possessed military, administrative and industrial ability worthy of that rank. In the early days Japan had had a foothold in Korea, and later had had contacts with the Koreans and the Chinese in the days of Hideyoshi in the 16th century; but these enterprises had failed owing to the lack of national strength and preparedness.

The diplomatic achievements of the Meiji Government accompanied the rapid internal development which it attained through the adoption of the Constitution and the establish-

ment of a new judicial system. For it was the straight-
forwardness of her foreign policy combined with this internal
development that induced Great Britain and the United States
of America to adopt a friendly attitude towards Japan. It
may also be that these countries regarded the growth of Japan
as a positive factor in the maintenance of peace and order in
the Far East. Thus after the Sino-Japanese War of 1894–95,
the Western powers, with Great Britain and the United States
playing a leading part, gradually recognized the unrestricted
status of Japan in the family of nations.

The fact that Japan attained national security and equality
with other nations chiefly by means of military and industrial
force has been of vital significance in her recent foreign policy,
and was caused fundamentally by the geographic, ethnic, and
economic factors contributing to the formation of the national
Japanese state and by the circumstances in which it was born.
This system was perpetuated in the parallel structure of the
civil and the military, under the sovereignty of the Emperor,
which characterized the Constitution of Japan. That military
strength played such a prominent part should not be lost sight
of in the understanding of the nature and development of
Japanese foreign policy, no matter what other interpretations
of her success may be given. It should be noted also that the
military gains and glory of the past fifty years have been such
as are likely to be long cherished by Japan—particularly since
the memory of her former miserable position before the strong
and arrogant Western powers is still vivid. At any rate, the
role of the military in the development of modern Japan has
been of paramount importance.

As time went on, however, and the international situation
altered, Japanese foreign policy gradually changed its method
as well as its goal. After Japan had freed herself of imminent
danger from the peninsula of Korea and South Manchuria

as the result of the Russo-Japanese War, her diplomatic
activities were devoted to consolidating her position in
Manchuria through negotiations with various countries. She
was successful as far as treaty making was concerned. For
the Anglo-Japanese Alliance was renewed, and continued to
be a pivot around which Japan's foreign policy revolved
until the Alliance was terminated at the Washington Conference. The Treaties with France and with Russia, providing for " spheres of interest " in Manchuria, were also concluded. This was indeed a period of imperialism, and as
the successor to the position formerly occupied by Russia,
Japan joined the group of imperialist nations. Industrially,
she had developed sufficiently to produce a capitalist class
which was interested in international cooperation with the
Western nations, with a view to carrying out the imperialistic
exploitation of China and other parts of Eastern Asia.

Japan's position in Manchuria, therefore, implied a new
orientation of her foreign policy. Now a land power on the
Asiatic continent as well as an empire-building sea power,
Japan was forced to seek and to develop her " spheres of
interest " while attempting to maintain a balance of power in
the Pacific as a whole, especially in the Far East. This new
aspect of her Asiatic policy she construed as a programme
maintaining special rights and interests in Manchuria. A
duality was now evident in her foreign policy : while she
cooperated in the general policy *vis-à-vis* China initiated by
the Western powers in the name of modern civilization, it
was nevertheless tacitly understood by the majority of the
Japanese people that she had special relations with the Asiatic
continent, upon which she depended for her economic security
and future prosperity, no matter what policies the Western
powers might pursue.

With the outbreak of the World War in 1914, the balance

of power in the Far East was suddenly upset. Japan's participation in the War, her demands upon China in 1915, and the Siberian Expedition in 1918 were important events which cannot be understood properly unless the duality in Japanese foreign policy is taken into due consideration. They clearly indicated what she was aiming at and how she directed her diplomatic activities. The temporary absence of the Western powers from the scene of the Far Eastern arena meant to Japan a retreat of her rivals and a removal of onerous pressure.

The World War saw the emergence of a new political force destined to be influential in the foreign as well as the domestic politics of the country—namely, the rise to power of the political parties together with the growth of the capitalist class. Having developed under bureaucratic and military tutelage, the political parties were generally nationalistic in their tenets, but critical of the government policies. However, since their position had been an irresponsible one for such a long time they were on the whole inexperienced in the conduct of international affairs. They had no real foreign policy of their own ; and, as subsequent history proved, it was a misfortune for Japan that in the wake of rapid industrialization, their voices as the representatives of the people should now suddenly have become decidedly influential in shaping the country's foreign policy.

The Far East of the post-War years was not the same as that of the pre-War period. The rapid progress of industrialization, the development of political consciousness on the part of the people at large, and the growth of social unrest heralded the emergence of a new Far East. Social forces and political trends of entirely new kinds were being created. Only a deep understanding of and a broad outlook on the international situation could have devised a new scheme of international adjustment applicable to this changed Far East.

The Washington Conference, like the Versailles Conference in the European field, was convened to settle problems concerning the Pacific area which had arisen during the War. A party government was then in power in Japan, which not only accepted the entire series of treaties proposed at the Conference, but showed a singularly passive attitude towards the Conference. Had she possessed a true understanding of the whole situation and sufficient exprience in conference diplomacy, Japan would have been in a position to take the initiative in proposing an international programme not only adapted to the new Far East, but conducive to her best advantage. It was, however, too gigantic a task for an Oriental nation. And there is always the possibility that the Western nations were eager to capitalize on this very inexperience of Japan.

The Washington treaties, especially the Nine-Power Treaty, did achieve a temporary peace in the Far East. But serious charges can be raised against them. In the first place, they embodied the idea that the Far East is essentially a place for the commercial and financial activities of the Western peoples ; and in the second, they emphasized the importance of placing the signatory powers on an equal footing, thus ignoring the desirability of providing for special relations between particular countries, especially between Japan and China. The American conception of the " Open Door " and equal opportunity, originating in British experiences in China, now came to be accepted as the guiding principle in the new Far East. If circumstances had allowed, Japan would have effected such appropriate modifications of this principle as would guarantee a truly durable peace. As it was, the Japanese business people, especially the bankers and the exporters of light-industry commodities, were quite as uncritical as the diplomats of the Foreign Office in accepting the formula of the Washington treaties, emphasizing the possibilities of Japanese trade with China. The liberal intellectuals were also enthusiastic about this policy because of its underlying idea of international cooperation. The support of the policy by these leading classes, however, was neither well-founded nor permanent. For they were unable to calculate the potentialities of the revolutionary changes in their part of the world; they lightly assumed that social and political trends in Far Eastern countries, especially in the old Empire of China, would resemble those of 19th century Europe. In short, they were not experienced enough to understand the implications of the Far Eastern situation.

The calculations of Japan, and of the Western powers also, with regard to peace and prosperity were soon to be entirely upset by the ascendancy in China of nationalism and its revolutionary diplomacy, the organized propaganda of the Communist International, the indignity inflicted upon Japan by the United States through the Immigration Law of 1924, and the severe economic depression which swept the whole world. These unexpected events and disagreeable problems aroused somewhat an acute reaction not only among the traditional die-hard nationalists and reactionaries, but even among the business people, the political parties and other liberal quarters in Japan. Consequently, the struggle between a " positive " versus a " conciliatory " policy vis-à-vis China became a political issue which divided public opinion. Instead of expounding at this point the development of this issue, which culminated in the Manchurian Incident of 1931, it may be sufficient to indicate that the selfish policies of the Western powers as well as the futile and indecisive foreign policy of the Japanese political parties were important causes of the subsequent rise in Japan of the militaristic and nationalistic movement.

The reversal of Japan's foreign policy was closely related to the changes taking place internally. The ill-timed programme of economy and deflation adopted by the Minseitō administration in 1930–31 aroused intense popular dissatisfaction, particularly among the farming and small-business classes which were severely hit by this orthodox policy. In fairness it must be said that the economic depression was not caused by this policy alone. The real cause perhaps lay deeper, in the economic and industrial structure of the country. But it is easy to understand why the people, in their desperate state of mind, should have been inclined to discredit the government policy of the day, and indeed the whole system of party government as well, in the belief that political parties were concerned fundamentally with their own private interests at the expense of the national welfare as a whole. On moral as well as institutional grounds, therefore, this political system was now brought to trial.

After the Manchurian Incident of 1931, the political ideology of the Japanese people as a whole underwent a radical transformation. In this new state of mind, the withdrawal from the League of Nations and from the Washington treaties was accepted with less reluctance, and with less fear of isolation, than would have otherwise been the case. The troubles in North China which began in 1931 were regarded by the Japanese people as a natural sequence of the Manchurian Incident.

The policy of making North China an autonomous buffer-region between Manchoukuo and China, although an inevitable result of the unrest there, had various and dangerous possibilities—a fact which was not taken into serious consideration by the Japanese people who did not fully appreciate the tremendous drive in China for national unification after the Manchurian Incident. This movement was indirectly supported by the League of Nations in general and, as exemplified in the case of the currency reform, by Great Britain in particular. Under the leadership of Chiang Kai-shek and with the support of the Western democratic powers which wanted to keep China in a semi-colonial state safe from the continental advance of the Japanese, China was rapidly becoming a military-fascist country, subduing most of the semi-feudal, antagonistic warlords and driving the Chinese Communist armies into the remote Northwest.

Now the Japanese people realized that a serious situation had been created. They knew that their China policy had encountered a great obstacle when diplomatic negotiations with the Nanking Government broke down to all intents and purposes. They realized that the anti-Japanese forces in China had gained uncontrollable momentum, when the Sian Incident soon led to Kuomintang-Communist cooperation.

Therefore, the outbreak of the North China Incident in the summer of 1937 was accepted by the Japanese people as the arrival of the inevitable. Although the Government quickly announced a policy of local settlement and non-aggravation, no one could expect that the affair would be ended in such a manner, in view of the preparedness and aggressive attitude of the Chinese Nationalist front. And, indeed, the North China Incident developed into a major clash which, though officially termed an incident, is in fact a war.

In the course of the conflict, after the occupation of the Canton and Wuhan areas, the Konoye Cabinet issued two statements : the first concerning the Japanese war aim, that is, the establishment of a New Order in East Asia, and the second concerning a more concrete policy for the adjustment of Sino-Japanese relations. It is now declared that Japan's aim is not to conquer China, or to take any territory from her, but instead to create jointly with China and Manchoukuo a new order comprising the three independent states. In accordance with this programme, East Asia is to become a vast self-sustaining region where Japan will acquire economic security and immunity from such trade boycotts as she has been experiencing at the hands of Western powers.

Whether this immense task will succeed, only the future can tell. That Japan should have imposed this task upon herself—that she should have turned in this direction—was perhaps only natural. For on the one hand, she had already withdrawn from most of the international peace systems, including the League of Nations Covenant and the Washington treaties, while on the other her relations with China had reached an impasse. Nor was it unreasonable for Japan to conclude the Anti-Comintern Pact with Germany and Italy, if for no other reason than her traditional attitude of seeking friendship with any nation, regardless of its political ideology, which appreciates her international position.

Such an attitude on the part of Japan does not at all mean a Japanese isolation from the rest of the world or non-cooperation with the democratic powers. On the contrary, Japan is seeking international cooperation ; only, she is seeking it on an entirely new basis. How such a basis can be agreed upon, and how the policies and interests can be adjusted, as between Japan and the Western powers will be the most important problem that has ever existed in the history of the Far East. But this much must be clear that the Western powers can contribute a great deal by becoming more realistic in their attitude towards the Japanese demands, broader in their outook of their own national interests in China, and more considerate in their activities so as to promote international justice among the peoples in the Far East. Now that Japan has for the first time since the Great War come to propose

a truly constructive policy for the Far East on her own initiative, the international peace of this part of the world in the
future will depend to a considerable extent on the responsive
and equally constructive attitude of the Western powers.

PART ONE

FROM THE 1914–18 WAR TILL THE
MANCHURIAN INCIDENT

CHAPTER I

JAPAN'S DIPLOMATIC ACTIVITY DURING THE WORLD WAR

Japan's Entry into the War

On August 23, 1914, having decided officially to participate in the World War, Japan declared war on Germany. The Japanese and the British Governments had exchanged views beforehand regarding the steps to be taken by Japan under the stipulations of the Anglo-Japanese Alliance, should Great Britain be drawn into the War. A formal British note requesting Japanese assistance in destroying German men-of-war in Chinese waters was addressed to the Japanese Government on August 7. One week later Japan sent a seven day ultimatum to Germany.

Contrary to the British request to limit her war operations to destroying the German naval forces in Chinese waters, Japan participated in the War in order to advance her own continental policy in the Far East. For she wanted to take this opportunity to solve the pending problems with China regarding Manchuria by destroying the German bases of operation in the Shantung Peninsula.

The notes exchanged between Tokyo and London show that there was a difference of opinion between the two Governments over the reason for Japan's entry into the War as well as over the extent of Japanese war operations. Although Great Britain wanted Japan to restrict her operations to destroying the German fleet in Chinese waters, she feared, on the basis of information furnished by her officials in China, that a Japanese declaration of war would cause disturbances in the entire Far

East and greatly injure British trade.   Since Japan persisted in her original decision, however, Great Britain finally agreed to the Japanese declaration of war, but declared unilaterally that the British Government understood that the sphere of Japanese war operations would not extend, except for the protection of her trade routes in the Pacific, beyond Chinese waters or beyond that part of the Asiatic continent in which German possessions were situated.

Concerning the precise grounds of Japan's entry into the War and the extent of her war operations, many interpellations were made in the thirty-fourth Diet, convened to approve the war budget.   Public sentiment found expression in a question by Diet members regarding the future of Kiaochow Bay.   On this important matter Count Katō, then Foreign Minister, answered consistently that Japan was under no commitment to England or any other power as to the restoration of Tsingtao and that no restrictions had been placed upon the sphere of operations of the Imperial Army and Navy.   Regarding the declaration of Great Britain referred to above, the Japanese Government stated that it was only a British interpretation of the intention of the Japanese Government.

It must be emphasized that Japan's entry into the War was determined fundamentally by her belief that the time had come for her to settle the whole problem of her position in China, especially in Manchuria—a settlement which had been thought to be increasingly necessary during the ten years after the Russo-Japanese War.   Owing to the negative policy adopted by successive administrations, economic and social conditions in Japan, especially in the agricultural districts, were critically serious.   Sooner or later Japan would have had to change her policies, and the World War was actually a heaven-sent opportunity.

The Sino-Japanese Negotiations of 1915

The " Twenty-One Demands ", which constituted the main subject of the Sino-Japanese negotiations of 1915, originated in a plan which Count Katō had formulated while Japanese Ambassador in London. The extension of the leases of the Kwantung Leased Territory and the South Manchuria Railway Zone was of great moment to Japan since her interests in Manchuria had become of paramount importance after the annexation of Korea in 1910. Although the preparatory conversation with Lord Grey had failed of any concrete result, Count Katō had awaited a chance to negotiate with China on this matter. He returned to Japan to become Foreign Minister in the Ōkuma Cabinet. While negotiating with London on the question of Japanese participation in the War, he was also instructing the Japanese Minister in Peking to open negotiations with China, and to urge President Yuan Shih-kai to place more confidence in Japan in view of the changing international situation.

The Cabinet and the Elder Statesmen agreed upon the principal demands to be presented to China, and decided to present them after the capture of Tsingtao. The terms, however, were not published, thanks to the strict censorship of the press. The original demands devised by Count Katō had been reasonable and moderate, with the primary intention of confirming Japan's " special position " in Manchuria. But once the decision to negotiate became known, many other demands were advanced by various quarters of political importance. Thus finally, the subject for negotiation was enlarged to comprise all twenty-one demands, classified in five principal groups.

With the fall of Tsingtao on November 7, 1914, the hitherto suppressed public opinion sought expression, and strong

views appeared in the press, advocating the solution of all
pending questions between Japan and China in addition to the
continued occupation of Kiaochow Bay and the extension
of the Japanese leased territories in Manchuria. Public excitement reached a state of frenzy over China's demand for
immediate withdrawal of Japanese troops from Tsingtao.
In this atmosphere Minister Hioki left for Peking on December
4, 1914, carrying final instructions.

The demands were presented directly to President Yuan
Shih-kai by the Japanese Minister on January 18, 1915. At
the ensuing conferences the Chinese representatives took a
very firm stand especially against the items in Group V, the
full acceptance of which, they thought, would have reduced
China to the position of a protectorate of Japan. Even in
Japan, despite the strength of public opinion, the wisdom of
presenting such demands had been doubted by a group of
persons who had sensed the general trend of public sentiment in China and elsewhere abroad. The Japanese Foreign
Minister insisted on striking out Group V, leaving these
demands for later negotiations, and he was successful in securing the consent of his Cabinet and the Elder Statesmen.
Thus on May 2, a revised list of demands, including the eventual
restoration of Kiaochow Bay to China, was presented to China
in the form of an ultimatum, which China accepted on May
9.

The Twenty-One Demands affair was a highly interesting
phase of Japanese diplomacy during the World War. Generally
it was criticized at home and abroad as a blunder. Japanese
public opinion, especially among the opposition parties in
the Diet, expressed dissatisfaction over the omission of Group
V ; it was essentially because of the revision of the original
demands and the weakness, as it was believed, of the Ōkuma
Cabinet in consenting to such revision that the whole affair

was called a blunder at home. Criticism abroad, however, was directed against what was considered the high-handedness or aggressiveness of Japanese diplomacy. It is noteworthy, therefore, that the affair created a very different impression in Japan and in the outside world.

In this connection it is interesting to note the inconsistent and contradictory grounds on which the opposition parties in the Diet attacked the Government. While they assumed a more demanding attitude towards China than the Government did in objecting to the omission of Group V and the promise of restoring Kiaochow Bay to China, in the same breath they considered that the time was not ripe for Japan to exert military pressure upon China, or to pursue negotiations which had aroused anti-Japanese feeling in China and unpopularity abroad. It was apparent that these politicians had no positive non-partisan programme of foreign policy, but simply more accustomed to changing their front in order to gain in power without seriously considering the consequences of their inconsistency. The diplomacy of Count Katō, which may have been a blunder, judged by the highest standard of diplomatic policy and technique, was nevertheless of value in the sense that it guided the nation without serious mistakes through a difficult situation.

Japan's Diplomatic Relations with the Allied Powers and the U.S.A.

It is instructive to trace the development of Japanese relations with the Allied Powers and the United States during the World War. Soon after the outbreak of the War the London Declaration of Alliance was signed by Great Britain, France and Russia. At the same time France and Russia formally invited Japan to conclude alliances with them. The Elder Statesmen were inclined to respond favourably to these proposals, particularly to that of a Russo-Japanese Alliance—a fact which revealed indirectly the traditional Japanese concern over Russo-Japanese relations.   Foreign Minister Katō, however, disagreed on the ground that the conclusion of such an important international treaty should be postponed until after the close of the War.   He was, perhaps, considering the effect of such a politically significant undertaking upon the British. He adhered consistently to the Anglo-Japanese Alliance as the polestar of Japanese Far Eastern policy, and declined a second proposal of France and Russia for a Four Power Alliance, for he believed that such an alliance would weaken the Anglo-Japanese Alliance.

After Count Katō had resigned and Viscount Ishii succeeded to the Foreign Ministership, Japan accepted a formal invitation of Great Britain on August 15 to adhere to the London Declaration ; and, after an exchange of notes between London and Tokyo, the Japanese Government formally became a party to it on October 19, 1915.

The contents of the negotiations were not submitted to the Privy Council for advice as in the case of a treaty or agreement requiring subsequent ratification.   In the opinion of the Government this procedure was not a violation of the Constitution or of the Privy Council organization ordinance.   In fact, the Cabinet was not in a position to make such a submission because the London Declaration and supplementary notes dealt with the understandings to be reached by the Allies regarding the proposed peace terms.   Such preliminary discussions among the Allied Powers took place in February and March 1917, and resulted in the secret agreements concerning the peace terms. In one of these agreements Great Britain promised to support the Japanese demand for the power of disposition of the German interests in the Shantung Peninsula and her possessions north of the equator.

The principal aim of Japanese foreign policy during the World War was the consolidation of her position in the Far East. It was because of this, that, in spite of the unfavourable attitude of foreign countries, Japan dared to grasp the opportunity to present the Twenty-One Demands in 1915. The same motive underlay her participation in the London Declaration. Further, Japan approached Russia, who was then in dire need of munitions and other materials, and proposed the fourth extension of the Russo-Japanese Agreement which had been one of the corner stones of Japanese Far Eastern policy. Some of the Elder Statesmen and other prominent statesmen were, as traditionally they had been, particularly in favour of this policy, because they realized that, in view of possible future Anglo-American ties, the Anglo-Japanese Alliance alone would not suffice to maintain Japan's position in the Far East. Nobody can tell what role the Russo-Japanese axis might have played in Far Eastern politics if the Russian Revolution had not broken out.

The Lansing-Ishii Agreement

Meanwhile in China relations between Japan and the United States were becoming strained. The great European powers—Germany, France, Great Britain and Russia—were preoccupied with the War, and international rivalries in China seemed to be restricted to that of Japan vs. America. A struggle ensued in Manchuria, where the Japanese had been successful in consolidating their bases of economic activity, and also in the main part of China, where Japanese influence had been extended after the Sino-Japanese Treaty of 1915. The United States Government was out to destroy the " spheres of interest " of all nations in China.

Japan determined to approach the American Government in respect to this " spheres of interest " problem and, therefore, sent a special mission under Viscount Ishii, with the ostensible purpose of congratulating America on her participation in the War.   As a result of ensuing conversations, the Lansing-Ishii Agreement was concluded on November 2, 1917, by which America recognized Japan's "special interest" in China and Japan signified her re-acceptance of the American policy of the Open Door.   While this agreement clearly embodied the sentiments of the people and the Government of Japan, it was unpopular in the United States.   It was finally terminated on April 14, 1923, by an exchange of notes between Secretary of State Hughes and Masanao Hanihara, the Japanese Ambassador in Washington.

The important point in regard to this short-lived agreement does not lie in the interpretation of the ambiguous meaning of " special interest ", whether political or economic, but in the fact that Japan claimed a special interest in China on the ground of her geographical position, and America, while accepting that much, stood at the same time opposed to any wider interpretation of the Japanese position in China, emphasizing the principles of the Open Door and equal opportunity.   Thus the problem could not be settled by such an agreement, since it was clearly apparent that the United States was not prepared to recognize the profound changes which had been taking place in the relations among the Far Eastern countries as a result of their industrial and cultural development.

The Siberian Expedition

The American proposal for a joint expedition to Siberia for the purpose of rescuing the Czechoslovakian troops was formally presented to the Terauchi Cabient on July 12, 1918. The Cabinet decided not only to accept the proposal of a joint expedition but also to dispatch an independent expedition

to carry out its own plan as originally conceived by a group
of the Elder Statesmen and military and financial interests.
This Cabinet plan, however, was opposed by a few members
of the Advisory Council on Foreign Relations, including Baron
Makino and Takashi Hara, President of the Seiyūkai party.
The leader of the Kenseikai party, Count Katō, had even
refused to enter the Advisory Council. Since the Cabinet's
project for an independent expedition was not approved by
either of the major parties in the Diet, the large-scale expedition originally planned had to be abandoned, but it
was stipulated that Japan would reserve freedom of action
for her troops, should defence operations become necessary.
After further communication with Washington, the Japanese
Government issued an important statement declaring that
it had accepted the American proposal for a joint expedition
and that it entertained no political or territorial designs on
Siberia.

Japan's Siberian expedition was dispatched without substantial national needs or popular support. It was natural,
therefore, that the Hara Cabinet which succeeded the Terauchi
Cabinet, the originator of this project, should have been
severely criticized by the opposition party when the forty-
first Diet opened. The Government answers to questions
on this matter were rather evasive and far from convincing.
Yet Japanese troops remained in Siberia even after the withdrawal of the American and other Allied troops in January
1920.

Meanwhile, the report on June 3, 1920, of the massacre
by Russians of over seven hundred Japanese soldiers and
civilians at Nikolaevsk in March and May aroused great
public excitement, and renewed the question of government
responsibility for the continued maintenance of the expedi-
tionary forces in Siberia. The Government, however, was

unable to evacuate troops from Russian territory, where the general situation remained unstable and the emergence of any responsible regime in Siberia favourable to Japan was unlikely.

While the government was thus in a difficult dilemma, bitter denunciation of the expedition, both in and out of the Diet, continued to grow. Finally a new Cabinet under Admiral Katō, the chief Japanese representative at the Washington Conference, announced the intended evacuation of troops from Siberia at the end of October 1922. Thus the unpopular Siberian expedition ended, having taught Japan the valuable object lesson that any project of political importance would not be successful unless it were backed by sufficient popular support.

CHAPTER II

THE PARIS PEACE CONFERENCE AND
THE WASHINGTON CONFERENCE

Japan at the Peace Conference

Though Japan's part in it was very small, the World War affected profoundly her place among the powers and socio-economic conditions at home. The temporary absence of European attention to economic and political affairs in the Far East, especially after Japanese participation in the War, was chiefly responsible for these changes. Japan seized the opportunity to increase her influence in China and to extend it to the South Seas. And since the trend of events in this part of the world had favoured the extension of Japanese influence even before the War, Japan considered herself entitled to induce the Western powers to revise their Far Eastern policies accordingly. Since, however, her participation in the War was rather unexpected, she was not quite prepared and her war time diplomacy was necessarily tinged with opportunism and even blundering. Nonetheless, by the time of the Peace Conference Japan had made some diplomatic and military gains requiring formal acknowledgment.

After final deliberations by the Advisory Council on Foreign Relations, the Japanese peace terms and demands to be presented at the Peace Conference were embodied in the instructions handed on December 8, 1918, to the Japanese delegation. The contents of the claims were discussed in both Houses, but the Cabinet consistently declined to reveal any of the policies involved.

Japan presented three major demands at the Peace Conference: *viz.*, the disposition of the German possessions north of the equator, the transfer of the German leasehold and other interests in the Shantung Peninsula, and the embodiment of "racial equality" in the Covenant of the League of Nations. The first two not only had been recognized already by the Allied Powers as early as 1915, but later had been accepted by China in the negotiations of 1915, and further reaffirmed by her after she had entered the War in 1918. Their acceptance was, therefore, virtually a foregone conclusion, at least in Japanese opinion. Japan had studied possible American reactions, particularly with respect to the Shantung problem and had determined that if America should refuse the Japanese claims, Japan would not enter the League of Nations. The question of "racial equality" was also one to which Japan had attached great importance to an extent scarcely appreciated in the West. Though it was deemed by some people to lack international political applicability, it really originated in the grievance of the Japanese towards the unequal treatments to which the coloured races were subjected by the Western peoples.

At the end of April, three months after the opening of the Conference, the Shantung question was solved. During the negotiations the Chinese delegates had constantly opposed the Japanese claims mainly on the ground of the invalidity of "unequal" treaties, in general, and of the Sino-Japanese Treaty of 1915, in particular. Supporting the Chinese delegates, the American members presented a twofold counter-proposal, but the Japanese steadfastly contended that unless their claims were accepted, they would not sign the treaty, an integral part of which was the Covenant of the League of Nations. Finally, though reluctantly, President Wilson gave in to the Japanese, when he discovered that they were resolved on this question. Accordingly, it was decided that

Germany's rights in Shantung should pass to Japan. The Japanese on their part declared that :

" The policy of Japan is to hand back the Shantung Peninsula in full sovereignty to China, retaining only the economic privileges granted to Germany and the right to establish a settlement under the usual conditions in Tsingtao."

On the whole the peace settlement itself and the Japanese programmes were not unpopular in Japan. The people, however, realized the true nature of international politics as epitomized in the Peace Treaty. As their understanding of world politics widened, their interest in diplomacy and foreign policy grew.

The Naval Limitation and the Four-Power Treaty

A discussion of the Japanese policy at the Washington Conference should emphasize the Japanese reaction to the information that an international conference might be convened by the United States. For the Japanese conception of the purpose of the Washington Conference differed from that of the other participants.

In the first place, with regard to the motive and scope of the Conference, the Japanese people understood that it was to be convened primarily with a view to restricting the naval armament race of the three principal naval powers—Great Britain, the United States and Japan—although the impossibility of such limitation without a certain reorientation of the foreign policies of these countries should have been apparent. Yet the Japanese were so preoccupied with the desirability of naval limitation itself that they did not seriously contemplate the possibility of a revision of their China policy. In fact, the Japanese people did not fully realize the political significance of the Washington Conference until the Manchurian Incident of 1931 ten years afterward.

Before the invitation to attend the Conference reached Japan, the question of a naval limitation conference had been widely discussed in the press. Baron Hayashi, Japanese Ambassador in London, was reported on January 20, 1921, to have freely alluded to such an international conference, although he was understood to have done so in a purely private capacity. In the forty-fourth session of the Diet, on January 22, 1921, Osachi Hamaguchi, a leading member of the Kenseikai party and later Prime Minister, requested Takashi Hara, the Prime Minister, to state the view of the Government on the possibility of a naval conference. Thus indirectly, the leader of the opposition party expressed the desirability of such a conference primarily from the stand-point of financial considerations. On February 10 Yukio Ozaki, a leading liberal and pacifist, introduced a resolution in the Lower House demanding a reduction of naval armament in concert with Great Britain and the United States, and of military armaments in accordance with the provisions of the Covenant of the League of Nations. Though the resolution was defeated by a vote of 285 to 88, owing to the opposition of both major parties in the Diet, Ozaki's campaign throughout the country for armament reduction received wide attention. The Japanese public was thus interested in a vague way in the idea of a new international political system without scrutinizing the harsh reality of the Pacific problem.

In the United States, however, the public as well as the Administration were determined to take this opportunity to restrain Japan's activities on the Asiatic mainland, and thus to maintain a balance of power in Eastern Asia. The Harding Administration apparently wished to extend American influence and prestige in Asia to counterbalance her retreat from Europe. In order to attain such Far Eastern policy, a navy strong enough to assure American supremacy in Pacific waters, appeared to be the order of the day. Propaganda had been spread throughout America to play up the "Japanese menace" in the Pacific. It was, however, not until the Stimson doctrine of non-recognition was announced in connection with the Manchurian Incident of 1931 that the political nature of this American Pacific policy was brought out in full relief.

American support of an international conference originated in a suggestion of the British Government, which must have considered Anglo-American cooperation more important than an Anglo-Japanese Alliance. There is ample evidence that Secretary of State Hughes acted upon Lloyd George's suggestion that the Conference should deal with the entire Far Eastern problem. Thus the announcement of the American Government in connection with the Conference read as follows : "It is manifest that the question of limitation of armament has a close relationship to the Pacific and Far Eastern problems." One may say that the Washington Conference was essentially a product of Anglo-American cooperation. Only history can tell whether it was fair to Japan.

Japan's instructions to her delegates showed that she was unaware of the political nature of the Conference. She confined her preparatory deliberations to the strategical and technical aspects of the problem of naval limitation. According to the press reports—no official announcement was made— the instructions embodied the following basic points : (1) Japan was prepared to accept a reduction of her naval armaments as long as her national security was not thereby impaired ; (2) she had no fortifications in her Pacific possessions which would threaten other countries, nor did she intend to create such establishments in the future ; moreover, she was prepared to conclude an agreement to abolish all military or naval bases and to promise also not to construct new ones in the Pacific ; (3) she did not wish to terminate the Anglo-

Japanese Alliance, but was not opposed to concluding a new alliance or agreement to replace it; (4) she was ready to extend the principles of the Open Door and equal opportunity to other nationals on the Island of Yap; (5) she was prepared to renew her assurances of the principles of equal opportunity and the Open Door in China; (6) she was determined to insist that the Shantung question be settled by direct negotiations between Japan and China, and to oppose any attempt at discussion of this matter in the Conference.

The debates in the forty-fourth session of the Diet revealed that the Japanese people, except for a small section of right-wing nationalists who were interested in Japanese expansion on the Asiatic mainland, did not fully appreciate the real significance of the Washington treaties, especially their bearings upon the future course of Japan's foreign policy. The interpellations centered on the reduction of naval armaments, and the Four-Power Treaty which had replaced the Anglo-Japanese Alliance, but conspicuously ignored the Nine-Power Treaty. This omission was not an evidence of satisfaction with the principles of that Treaty, but rather of insufficient knowledge of international politics in China.

The Washington treaties, particularly the naval reduction treaty, were received favourably by Japanese governmental circles partly because of the personality of the late Admiral Katō who led the Japanese delegates to the Conference, and partly because of the general opinion, expressed in the press as well as in the Diet, that the treaties would not only relieve international tension in the Pacific, but would also reduce the burden of taxation.

The Nine-Power Treaty

When it became known that discussions of Far Eastern problems would be included in the agenda of the Washington

Conference, the Government as well as the public of Japan entertained considerable doubt about the intentions of the United States, and expressed a marked reluctance to have their position in the Far East reviewed in such a manner. This hesitation was interpreted in various ways both in America and England; the opinion of the majority seemed to be that Japan was " too determined to pursue her own line of action to waste time discussing it ", or that Japan always preferred bilateral to multilateral negotiations in the hope of playing one Western nation off against another. Nothing could have been farther from the truth, which was that Japan at that time was simply not prepared for this method of handling the China problem. The political parties, then dominating the politics of the country, were equipped with neither experience nor knowledge sufficient to meet such a situation. Their political ascendancy had not been won through merit, but had been due to the turn of the political tide and the discrediting of the old military and bureaucratic elements. The people at large on their part were concerned only with securing a livelihood in that somewhat unstable era of reconstruction and readjustment. And before the intellectuals there loomed a vague idea of a new internationalism, too idealistic to be practicable. In such an atmosphere the Government could not fail to take a negative or skeptical attitude towards the conference method of dealing with Far Eastern problems.

The Washington Conference was a complete triumph of American diplomacy over Japanese. In accordance with their carefully prepared programmes, the American delegates examined the whole problem of the Far East at the conference table and, on almost every controversial point, succeeded in defeating the Japanese delegation, which was poorly equipped with civilian statesmen and experts on Far Eastern problems.

Baron Shidehara, Japanese Ambassador in Washington and career diplomat with no special knowledge of China, alone fought a defensive "battle" for the Japanese "special interest" in China, against the broad principles of the Open Door and equal opportunity. With practically no prepared data at hand, the delegation could not justify Japanese expansion on the Asiatic mainland, or induce the Americans to consider more soberly Japan's position in the Far East. The so-called four principles in China, which were duly incorporated in the Nine-Power Treaty, were merely the full embodiment of the traditional American Far Eastern policy since the day of John Hay. That Japan would accept the principles of the Open Door and equal opportunity may have been a foregone conclusion, but if she had been aware then of her own long term designs in China and had known how to define them, she would not have had to accept so passively the whole plan as proposed by America.

Since it may be argued that for Japan the Nine-Power Treaty was a signal diplomatic defeat, the reason underlying her signature of a treaty that would impede her natural continental expansion must be explained. If Japan had accepted it simply because refusal to acknowledge the Open Door would have been taken as indisputable proof of aggressive designs on China, then she would have been only Machiavellian. If she had acquiesced before the superior American Navy, then the Nine-Power Treaty would have been meaningless. Clearly neither consideration was decisive. In 1922, Japan was devoting most of her energy politically and economically to consolidating internally her gains of war. She looked to frictionless international relations to maintain her position in China and in the Far East, without seriously considering the existence of various contradictory elements in her own social structure, as well as conflicting forces in China, which would prove obstacles to the attainment of her objective. Criticism must also be directed at the Americans who were eager to compel Japan to accept their general principles without conceding her any special advantage with which she could develop her position in the Far East in an orderly fashion. Herein lay the fundamental weakness of the Washington Conference, as later history clearly revealed.

The Aftermath of the Washington Conference

Japan was faithful to the letter and spirit of the Washington treaties and agreements. Under the leadership of the Prime Minister, Admiral Katō, she began to scrap those capital ships whose abandonment was required by the naval treaty. In addition she concluded a Sino-Japanese postal agreement, resumed successful negotiations with China over the return of Shantung, and undertook the effective evacuation of her troops from Siberia. Japan's obliging attitude gave every reason to believe that the tension which had characterized American-Japanese relations prior to the Conference had now been completely cleared. And the efforts of the executive circles in both countries to this end must not be overlooked.

These seemingly friendly American-Japanese relations were, however, suddenly strained in 1924 by the issue of the Immigration Law. The new Law which was intended to halt the immigration of Japanese, was adopted largely at the instigation of traditional anti-Japanese elements in California and advocated simply for reasons of local, selfish expediency. It was unfortunate for both countries that the undiplomatic expression, "the grave consequences", used by the Japanese Ambassador Hanihara, should have been utilized by American politicians in Congress as a compelling argument for the necessity of immediate action to restrain Japan. Thus the law to exclude Japanese immigrants from the United States was passed, according to one American critic, owing to " persistent agitation, inadvertently abetted by diplomatic ineptitude and culminating in Senatorial hysteria ".

Japanese public opinion was so shocked and embittered that a wave of bitter anti-American sentiment spread throughout the country. Even the late Dr. Nitobe, who was a sincere friend of America, was so angry with the manner of the passage of the law that he cried : " I will never cross the Pacific Ocean again ". However, a serious crisis was prevented by the exercise of moderation and by executive efforts to reduce the reaction on both sides of the Pacific. It was not the substance of the policy of excluding Japanese immigrants—itself not a serious menace to Japan—but rather the psychological effect upon the Japanese that caused the Immigration Law to undermine fatally American-Japanese amity which had been one of the most important achievements of the Washington Conference. Thereafter, it is not too much to say, Japan turned her back on the collective system of diplomacy, and, as a natural corollary of her distrust of foreigners, the campaign of " Asia for the Asiatics " was vigorously revived among the traditional continentalists in Japan.

CHAPTER III

THE CHINA POLICY AND THE POLITICAL PARTIES

The Shidehara Policy and Its Conditions

After the Washington Conference, Japanese diplomacy continued loyally along the lines of the post-War collective system of international peace as embodied in the League of Nations Covenant and the Washington treaties. Succeeding the Katō and the Yamamoto Cabinets, a coalition of the three major parties was formed in 1924. Having passed the manhood suffrage bill, a long awaited hope for the liberal democracy in Japan, the coalition Cabinet was replaced in 1925 by a single party Cabinet of the Kenseikai, in which Baron Shidehara retained the post of Foreign Minister. Because he himself was one of the staunchest supporters of this principle, the Japanese foreign policy which favoured collective security after the Washington Conference is generally known as the Shidehara policy.

Diplomacy of this kind, however, could continue in Japan only under certain conditions. A conciliatory attitude on the part of Japanese public opinion towards China, combined with commercial gains for Japanese business through peaceful penetration into China on the basis of cooperation between the two nations, was one set of such conditions. Another was a concert of policy and action on the part of the powers, interested in China, which would enable the liberals in Japan to maintain their popularity among, and secure the confidence of the masses. Upon these circumstances the Shidehara policy depended for its success.

Baron Shidehara, as Foreign Minister in the Minseitō (renamed Kenseikai) Cabinet, formulated his China policy on the assumption that the Japanese national economy which had been inflated during the War could neither maintain its *status quo* nor nourish the contemporary level of prosperity unless more outlets were found in China, and that consequently the China policy of Japan should be pursued more earnestly than that of other powers in the direction of allaying Chinese ill-will. He was indeed a nationalist in the true sense of the term, although by his opponents in the country he was designated as a " weak " liberal in his method of diplomacy.

His assumption of the trends and needs of the Japanese national economy cannot be discarded simply as a mistake arising from class bias. It must be recalled that the World War encouraged the industrialization of Japan and created a huge market for her industrialists and farmers. Not only did Russia and other Allied powers look to Japan for their munitions and other war supplies, but the Oriental countries and the South Seas, cut off from former European sources of supply, turned to Japan for a wide range of manufactured goods. The War disrupted world industry and shipping ; it freed Japan, for the time being, from European competition at home and opened to Japanese trade the markets of the Asiatic mainland and the South Seas previously served by European manufactures. It followed, therefore, that the restoration of peace and the revival of competition was a severe blow to the Japanese national economy which had been enlarged during the War. Hence the maintenance and promotion of the China trade was deemed to be of the utmost importance for Japan, and the Shidehara policy was naturally conditioned by this domestic situation.

It appears, then, that Baron Shidehara's China policy was based upon certain fundamental principles : (1) to respect the sovereignty and territorial integrity of China, and to uphold the policy of non-interference in her domestic affairs ; (2) to promote peaceful co-existence and economic cooperation between China and Japan ; (3) to regard reasonable national aspirations of China with sympathy and good will and to aid her in a cooperative manner to realize them ; (4) to maintain an attitude of patience and toleration towards the existing situation in China and, at the same time, to do the utmost to protect Japan's rights and interests in China, with reasonable measures. That this was Baron Shidehara's policy was made evident by his instructions to the Japanese Minister in Peking and the Consul-General in Mukden, in connection with the civil strife between the Mukden and Chihli factions in September 1925, to notify both factions fully to respect Japanese rights and interests in Manchuria. In the case of the Kuo Sung-ling Affair in November 1925, the same warning was given to the belligerent factions not to carry on warlike operations within the three-mile zone along the South Manchuria Railway. Though his attitude was a negative one, Baron Shidehara was earnest in protecting Japan's special position in Manchuria.

With respect to international cooperation with China in accordance with the resolutions adopted at the Washington Conference, specifically at the powers' conference with reference to the problem of tariff autonomy and extraterritoriality, his policy was not altogether tactful. The Japanese delegates proposed to recognize the tariff autonomy of China, forestalling other delegates, and yet in fact, as the actual proceedings of the conference showed, Japan was the last country to recognize the essential tariff autonomy of China. Owing to such contradictory actions on the part of Japan in addition to the British objection to the Japanese proposals for the aboliiton of *likin*, the appropriation of increased revenues to consolidate the national debts and the establishment of a reciprocal tariff-rate, the tariff conference broke up in July 1926. This episode proved that in handling the China problem Shidehara was really considering his country's own interests rather than international conciliation.

The Shidehara policy, however, was criticized severely by the opposition forces in Japan at the time of the Nanking Incident of 1927, when fighting by the revolutionary army of the Kuomintang caused large loss of life and property among foreigners, including the property of Japanese. Baron Shidehara refused to send troops to rescue and protect Japanese residents at that time. It is owing to such a liberal attitude that his policy was regarded as " weak ". Unpopularity arising from such causes hastened the downfall of the Minseitō Government, with a Seiyūkai Cabinet headed by Baron Tanaka succeeding it on April 17, 1927.

The Tanaka Policy and Its Background

The Minseitō Government was overthrown not only for its China policy, but also because of Privy Council's opposition to an emergency Imperial Ordinance prepared by the Cabinet to rescue the Bank of Taiwan from a threatening financial crisis.

The Seiyūkai Cabinet which succeeded was headed by General Tanaka as Premier and Foreign Minister. Upon forming the Cabinet, Baron Tanaka, with a view to formulating a " new China policy," summoned a conference of representatives of the Foreign, Finance, War and Navy Departments, the General Staffs of both military services, the head of the Kwantung garrison, the Japanese Minister to China and three important Consuls-General stationed in China and Manchuria. This conference lasted from June 27 to July 7, 1927 and was known as the " Far Eastern Conference ". Views and opinions of the participants were divergent, but the general tone was reported to favour a more " positive " policy *vis-à-vis* China than that followed by the previous Cabinet. In emphasizing the difference in policies to be pursued towards China proper and towards Manchuria and Eastern Inner Mongolia, Premier Tanaka was reported to have declared that " Japan has a responsible duty in making the Three Eastern Provinces of Manchuria safe for the settlement of foreign people as well as for the natives ".

Since the Nanking Incident and the advance in influence of the Chinese Nationalist movement in the North, the Japanese public had begun to entertain doubts about the policy which the country had pursued towards China. However, they were not prepared unconditionally to endorse Tanaka's new China policy, which was essentially a product of the vacuum created by the temporary failure of the Shidehara policy. It had, however, a strong point : it found support in the traditional public feeling that the Japanese special interests in Manchuria were to be distinguished from those in other parts of China. Specifically Baron Tanaka wished to develop his policy by consolidating or promoting projects of railroad extension, land tenure rights, trade in the interior of Manchuria, and the like. The intervention in the form of the dispatch of troops into the Shantung area in the spring of 1927 may be construed as a positive warning to China of his intention to protect Manchuria from the advance of the Nationalist movement.

By the beginning of April 1928 Chinese Nationalist forces had advanced far in their march to " subjugate the North " and Marshal Chang Tso-lin, war lord of Manchuria and also master of Peking, had joined them. His position had thus become perilous ; in fact his withdrawal from northern China seemed unavoidable in the face of Japanese intervention. If, however, his withdrawal meant an extension of the political influence of the Chinese Nationalists into Manchuria, it would be detrimental to Japan's position and interests there. The time looked ripe for the Tanaka Cabinet to launch its " positive " policy. After a series of preliminary conferences between the Cabinet and the Army regarding the grave situation near Tsinan, Premier Tanaka, the War and the Navy Ministers decided on the morning of April 18 to dispatch an immediate expedition to Tsinan. An extraordinary meeting of the Cabinet was called on the following morning, when General Shirakawa, Army Minister, and Admiral Okada, Navy Minister, first reported on the situation in China. After brief deliberation upon the matter, the meeting formally approved the immediate dispatch of troops to the threatened area in China. On the next evening (April 20) an official announcement was made, disclaiming any intention to interfere with the domestic affairs of China or to favour one faction against another, and declaring the intention of withdrawing the troops as soon as the security of the Japanese residents was assured.

That the Tsinan expedition was planned and carried out without the unanimous support of even responsible quarters was shown in the discrepancies in opinion between the officials stationed in Tsinan and those in the Kwantung territory in Manchuria and between the Cabinet as a whole and the General Staff. In such a confused situation, the responsibility of Baron Tanaka as Premier and Foreign Minister became increasingly heavy in the face of the hostile parliamentary opinion led by the Minseitō against the " partisan " policy of the Cabinet. Moreover, the expedition itself proved by no means effective in attaining its primary objective of protecting the lives and property of the Japanese residents. Baron Shidehara was right when in the House of Peers he charged the Cabinet with conducting the China policy for partisan purposes and domestic effect. But he was short-sighted in confining his interpellation to the defence of his own policy at the time of the Nanking Incident—at that time the safety of Japanese residents was maintained without dispatching a single soldier —and not referring more concretely to the broader aspects of Japanese policy *vis-à-vis* China.   The real problem was the manner in which Japan was to deal with the Chinese Nationalist movement, and its repercussions upon the relations between Japan and Manchuria.   Baron Shidehara and his party entirely neglected this important aspect of the problem.

Baron Tanaka was clumsy in prosecuting his positive policy, especially in dealing with the consequences of the Tsinan Incident.   Naturally the Tanaka policy became very unpopular, if for no other reason than the repeated dispatch of troops. At that time Japan was not in a mood to fight against the army of the Nationalist Government for the sake of some remote apprehension about her future position in Manchuria.   On the contrary, she felt the necessity of settling the pending problems created by the Hankow and Nanking Incidents with a view to recognizing ultimately the Nanking Government as the legitimate central Government of China.   Thus under the pressure of public opinion then prevailing in Japan, the Tanaka Cabinet was finally obliged to negotiate with the representatives of the Nanking Government in regard to the Tsinan Incident.   The negotiations reached the stage for the representatives of both parties to sign a provisional agreement, including the terms of the withdrawal of troops. After the episode of Premier Tanaka's blunder, when he sent his instructions without placing the matter before the Privy Council, the Tanaka Cabinet eventually succeeded in obtaining the approval of the Privy Council and the Imperial sanction to sign the agreements on the three incidents.   Formal signatures were attached to the notes on May 2, and these notes were made public on May 6, 1929.   Two months later the Tanaka Cabinet resigned and was replaced by a

Minseitō Cabinet.

In conlcuding this chapter, it seems appropriate to add a few words on the nature of Baron Tanaka's positive policy. This policy, which is generally regarded as a complete failure, failed chiefly because of his lack of executive ability in dealing with the turbulent situation caused by the advance of the Kuomintang Government. The allegation often made by foreign writers concerning the death of Marshal Chang Tso-lin may be regarded to a large extent as a by-product of his clumsinesses shown elsewhere. For example, he sent Baron Gonsuke Hayashi, former Ambassador to Great Britain, to " advise " the son of Chang Tso-lin, Chang Hsueh-liang in Mukden. This young war lord had changed his father's policy towards the central Government of China and had become more conciliatory towards the Kuomintang. Although this shift was a serious matter for Japan, Baron Tanaka might have acted more discreetly. Despite these shortcomings, he was right in sensing instinctively that the growth of Nationalist movement in China and the traditional policy of Japan in Manchuria and Inner Mongolia were irreconcilable, and he was farsighted in recognizing the advisability of checking the tide in Manchuria which had begun to flow with increasing vigour towards the Nationalist Government.

CHAPTER IV

THE LAST PHASE OF PARTY GOVERNMENT AND INTERNAL CRISIS

The Growth of Party Politics after the World War

The international policy of a nation is as susceptible to ideological influences as are domestic politics. The post-War period in Japan was characterized by the growth of representative government and party politics, a phenomenon which is most conspicuous in modern Japan, and its bearing upon the foreign policy of this period was naturally considerable.

The political parties in Japan had to undergo a period of some thirty years of " apprenticeship " before they were able to assume a position of leadership. The framers of the Constitution probably intended that the Government should always be in the hands of clan statesmen and bureaucrats, and for a time the party politicians were prevented from taking any part in the actual work of legislation and administration under the Constitution. Bureaucratic statesmen, however, gradually became convinced that, no matter how distasteful it might be, an alliance with one or the other of the dominant parties in the Lower House was both necessary and desirable in order to avoid disturbance in state affairs. They began to offer portfolios in the Cabinet to the leaders of the parties, but this did not mean that the principle of ministerial responsibility to Parliament was recognized. The political parties did not insist on this principle and were satisfied with whatever advantages they secured from such an arrangement. In this way an understanding based on a compromise between bureaucracy and political party emerged before the Russo-Japanese

War. Such bureaucratic and military leaders as Prince Itō and Prince Katsura became themselves leaders of political parties in order to facilitate the management of state policy.

The two major parties of Japan were originally under the tutelage of the bureaucratic and military leaders. With such a background, it was inevitable for the parties to become personal coteries easily influenced by the Government. Under the Constitution, no progress might not have been possible without some sort of compromise, but the period of the alliance between political parties and bureaucrats was the beginning of the widespread political corruption that did so much to bring pre-War domestic politics into disrepute.

In view of the domestic situation, the sudden post-War ascendancy of the political parties, leading to the emergence of party government, was an unexpected phenomenon and was due to the fact that the World War had given the political parties a hitherto undreamed-of opportunity for activity and responsibility. Rapid industrial development, commercial expansion, and the influx of democratic ideology from the West all accelerated the rise to power of the parties, finally bringing about the formation of a party government. In 1919 the Seiyūkai party, headed by Takashi Hara, organized the first single-party Cabinet in Japanese history. The people at large rejoiced at this event, as if it were a victory for democracy, and there followed a period of some ten years of party government.

The power of the political parties were depended in the last analysis upon the economic prosperity created by the World War. They naturally interested themselves in internal development, that is, the domestic redistribution of the economic gains accumulated through the expansion of Japanese trade and industry. Specifically they endeavoured, on the one hand, to gain popular support by giving grants to the local governments to assist in public works, education and other public services. For this purpose they sought legislation and appropriations for the construction of railways, highways, bridges, harbours, school buildings and the like. On the other hand, whether in power or in the opposition, they were in close contact with leading financial concerns like the Mitsui and Mitsubishi and other industrial concerns, and were supplied with election funds in return for general or particular favours. They were also connected with local landlords and business men of local influence, helping these people to advance their interests in return for support received from them in establishing and promoting the local party organizations.

The only substantial difference in the domestic politics of Japan between the pre-War and post-War eras was that formerly the Governments of the country had been almost monopolized by bureaucratic clansmen while after the War the majority of Cabinet posts was held by party men. With regard to readiness to take full advantage of the powers granted them, these party men proved themselves to be not one whit more modest than their bureaucratic predecessors. The successive party Governments were, in fact, never democratic in the full sense of the term. As far as the representation of the nation's wishes was concerned, the change from a bureaucratic to a party government was, therefore, a change in name rather than in spirit. The party Governments not only neglected entirely the welfare of the "forgotten man", but did not grasp the fundamentals of democratic government. The two major parties differed little in their platforms or policies; both were concerned mainly with a struggle for power.

When the universal manhood suffrage bill, which had been passed in 1925, was put into effect for the first time in Japan during the general election of 1928, 500,000 votes were cast for the proletarian parties, and eight members belonging to these parties were elected to seats in the Diet. Owing to a lack of unity, however, these parties did not continue to grow, and in the subsequent elections they did not command so many votes as had been anticipated. Generally speaking, their camp was split into radical and moderate elements, and the latter, though more popular, were too weak to assume the leadership of the whole farming and working class movement.

In those days the Japanese political parties, including the proletarian parties, were groups of factions of men whose interest and knowledge were confined to domestic politics. They singularly neglected to concern themselves with international affairs, an oversight which was fatal to the maintenance of their position in politics. They left the shaping of foreign policy to the bureaucrats and militarists, and tried to reap the harvest without having sowed the seed. It was only natural, therefore, that their hegemony should have been destroyed the moment a new situation arose on the international horizon.

The Agricultural Crisis and the Plight of the Japanese National Economy

In spite of their fundamental weakness, the political parties were able to engage in domestic politics with safety as long as no material change took place in the economic and financial situation of the country, which, essentially unsound though it was, appeared prosperous as a result of the gold embargo and an inflated price level. Gradually it became clear, however, that Japan could not enjoy this economic legacy of the War indefinitely, for unmistakable signs of economic and financial depression had begun to appear in various quarters.

It was over the financial and industrial policy purporting to cope with the economic depression that, in the last phase of party government, a fierce division of opinion occurred between the major parties. For the first time in the history of the parties, reference was made to international politics or economic doctrines in order to solve a national problem. Though it did so too late, the Minseitō led by such prominent persons as Hamaguchi, Shidehara and Inouye, launched a campaign for economy and deflation in accordance with the orthodox economic theory. It carried out a drastic economy in expe   ~res throughout all the government departments and lif   'd embargo in January 1930.

T'   'icy gave big industrial and banking
in   " rationalize " their obsolete organi-
                    industries—notably the rayon
                    It removed a check upon
                    ization of international
                    lities. But, on the whole,
                    agriculture. For the return
                    y impeded the small exporting
                    the price level so that small
                    tural class bacame unable to pay
                    t of their reduced incomes. On
                    s could not accommodate themselves
                    policy of the Government, and they
be.   y government system was being manipu-
lated ʋ,   ancial and industrial groups to serve their
interests a.   The opposition party and other political
groups joined forces in stirring up people, but in so doing they only added to the discredit of the political parties as a whole. The Minseitō Government failed to survive the popular reaction to its policy, and resigned in 1931. But the Seiyūkai Government which succeeded was not only unable to restore its damaged prestige to the political parties, but was fated, as subsequent history proved, to suffer an even

severer blow, for on the Asiatic mainland various forces were gathering slowly but steadily towards the outbreak of a great event which was completely to alter Japanese politics, internal as well as international.

The disrepute which the farmers brought upon the political parties was perhaps their greatest setback. Agriculture is still the chief industry of the country, though because of the development of manufacture and trade since the World War its role in the economic structure of the nation has been halved. It is still the most important industry on two accounts, as it provides the livelihood of half of the population, and the principal food supply of the entire nation. During the past fifty years the area of land under cultivation has increased about twenty-five per cent, while the population has more than doubled. Any deficiency in the food supply was made up partly through intensive and improved methods of cultivation, thanks to which the rice crop has been more than doubled during the past half century, and partly by the import of rice from colonial possessions and other parts of the mainland of Asia. As long as the production of the domestic rice fell short of the national consumption, the farmers naturally concentrated upon rice cultivation, making it their chief source of income. They were contented, therefore, as long as the price of rice tended to rise because of the increasing demand, and in that sense rice was regarded as an index of prosperity. Naturally a policy advocating a higher price for rice was encouraged by the political parties whose constituencies were controlled by a majority of the farming population.

This situation changed after 1925, when the price of rice began to decline, and declined faster and farther than the prices of other commodities. Generally speaking, the main cause was the general decline in prices, but there were also special causes. One was an over-production of domestic rice, and another was an excessive import of rice from colonial possessions, particularly from Chōsen. Yet, so long as the political parties were in power no policy of restricting such import was practicable.

The political parties finally proved to be unable to control the price of rice, and it was out of their incompetency that the "new bureaucracy" arose. The retrenchment policy and the return to the gold standard effected by the Minseitō Government, in conjunction with an abundant rice crop, helped to bring about a particularly severe fall in the price of rice. Eventually a governmental price control board was established in order to stabilize the price of rice by administrative measures. The device adopted by this board was to set a criterion by which to control the price. Actually, by means of higher mathematics applied to indices of the trend of the market price of rice, costs of production and costs of living, upper and lower limits were determined for an "official" price. On the one hand, the Government was obliged to buy rice from whoever wished to dispose of it at a price within the limits thus set, even if the market price was below the lower limit. On the other, the rice thus bought and stored had to be sold at a price within the limits, even if the market price were higher than the upper limit. In the former case the government purchase saved the farmers from suffering from a low price; in the latter, the government sale benefited the consumers while not injuring the farmers who enjoyed a higher price. This policy, designed to stabilize the rice price, worked satisfactorily on the whole, but it brought credit to the bureaucracy rather than to the political parties.

In addition to the problem of rice, that of the silk industry was equally important. Mainly because of the falling price of silk caused by the depression in America, together with the return to the gold standard in Japan, and partly because of the development of rayon manufacture as a substitute for natural silk, severe damage was inflicted upon agricultural regions where sericulture and silk-reeling flourished as a subsidiary industry. For the solution of this problem the Government adopted various adminstrative devices like nationalization of cocoon seeds and control by the method of cartelization of sericulturists, silk-reelers, wholesale merchants and exporters. As in the case of rice, these devices of control only enhanced the power and prestige of the bureaucracy, to the detriment of the political parties which had neither the administrative technique nor the expert knowledge required for the management of national economy.

CHAPTER V

THE PACT FOR THE OUTLAWRY OF WAR AND THE LONDON NAVAL TREATY

The Pact of Paris Controversies

Throughout the period of party government in Japan (1919–1931) as described in the preceding chapters, no fundamental change took place in her international policy in spite of much turbulence in her domestic affairs. All of the successive party Cabinets, the Minseitō and the Seiyūkai alike, adhered to the system of collective security. Unmistakably, however, a current had appeared which, side by side with the anti-Western element traditional in Japan, flowed in a contrary direction; and, in the last phase of the period now under survey, it began to assert itself with increasing vigiour, although the party leaders continued to make their country's policy conform to the post-War principle of international collective security advocated by the United States and Great Britain. Public opinion on the whole continued to favour collective security.

In April 1928 when General Baron Tanaka was Premier and Foreign Minister in the Seiyūkai Cabinet, Japan was formally approached by the American Government with reference to her participation in the Kellogg-Briand Pact for the renunciation of war. After careful examination of the American proposal by the Foreign Office and other important quarters and subsequent approval by the Cabinet, the Japanese Government replied affirmatively to the American inquiry on May 26. This reply read in part: " The proposal of the United States is understood to contain nothing that would refuse to independent states the right of self-defence, and nothing which is incompatible with the obligation of agreements guaranteeing the public peace, such as those embodied in the Covenant of the League of Nations and the Treaties of Locarno."

The second formal American draft was transmitted to the Japanese Government on June 23, 1928. In this draft the phraseology, " in the names of their respective peoples ", was found to be incompatible with the provisions of the Japanese Constitution, and consequently Japan asked the United States to amend the phraseology or to remove it from the text. To do this, however, the latter expressed reluctance on the ground that such an amendment might lead to endless negotiations and endanger the conclusion of the Pact itself, and argued that the phraseology in question did not contain any legal meaning objectionable to Japan. After exchanging notes on the interpretation of the phraseology in question, Japan decided to agree to the text of the Pact and dispatched the following memorandum on July 16, 1928:

> " It is understood that the phrase ' in the names of their respective peoples ' in Article I of the draft for the Outlawry of War does not signify ' as the agents of their peoples '; namely, that it is not the peoples themselves who conclude this treaty and that the phrase in question has been inserted in the Treaty for the purpose of impressing upon the peoples the importance of the renunciation of War. "

After receiving an American memorandum with reference to this Japanese interpretation, Japan formally agreed to sign the Treaty on July 20.

As to the phraseology in question, both public and parliamentary opinions were rather divided. Some people blamed the Government for not having offered an amendment to the text. Viscount Ishii, Yukio Ozaki and other prominent persons maintained that the phraseology was incompatible with the Constitution, that it was an encroachment upon the treaty-making as well as the war-making power of the Emperor, and that the Pact should not be ratified without reservation. Others, including an array of learned jurists, supported the contention of Premier Tanaka that the phraseology was interpreted to mean that " the Emperor declared on behalf of the state ", and argued that it was not intended to indicate the location of sovereignty and that the Pact was clearly within the letter and spirit of the Constitution.

As to the substance of the Pact, there were some interpellations in the Diet which inquired into the relation of the Pact to self-defence, and especially its bearing upon Japan's policy in Manchuria and Inner Mongolia. Premier Tanaka took this opportunity to state the Government's position and declared clearly that Manchuria was within the field covered by self-defence; if disturbances should occur in Manchuria which might threaten peace and order, Japan would be compelled, and have the right to take necessary measures—an action which could not be considered a violation of the Pact.

As far as the Pact of Paris was concerned, the Tanaka Government did not make so serious a blunder as was asserted by some of the Minseitō members who wanted to use the controversy over the text of the Pact to their own advantage. It was proved, however, that the Government had been too hasty in sending Count Uchida to Paris to sign the Pact. For not only those party politicians in whose view party interest was more important than that of the nation, but the Privy Council through its influential members registered disapproval of such an action by the Government. Faced with this opposition, the Government changed its mind and decided to ratify the Pact with a reservation by which it was made clear that the phrase " in the names of their respective peoples " did not have any effect so far as Japan was concerned because of the provisions of the Imperial Constitution. The same attitude was adopted by the Privy Council, and the Emperor finally ratified the Pact with this reservation.

Immediately after the defeat of the Government in the Privy Council on June 26, Count Uchida tendered his resignation, and the Tanaka Government fell on July 2.

The London Naval Treaty and the Constitutional Crisis

Upon the fall of the Seiyūkai Cabinet of Baron Tanaka, a Minseitō Cabinet was formed again. The fall of the Tanaka Government had been partly a result of partisan politics typical of Japanese parties. There seemed to be little reason to expect that the Minseitō Government would be successful in removing partisan politics from foreign policy.

The positive China policy of the Tanaka Cabinet had really been fruitless as well as unpopular. The political situation in Manchuria was becoming increasingly complicated. Despite the " advice " of Baron Tanaka, Chang Hsueh-liang followed his own independent counsel, declaring allegiance to the Nanking Government in December 1928, and received the latter's commission as Commander-in-Chief of the North-Eastern Frontier Army, and as head of the Government of Manchuria and Jehol. In the spring of 1929, as the writer observed in person, there sprang up in Manchuria numerous Chinese organizations in connection with the Kuomintang Nationalist movement. In short, the Nationalists threatened to wean Manchuria away from Japan.

Neutrality in the controversy of 1929 between Russia and the Chinese ruler in Manchuria might appear to have been an appropriate policy for Japan, but actually it was the result of an indecisive attitude as well as poor tactics. Japan was then suffering not only from party quarrels, but from a lack of unity among her political leaders. Despite its failure to dislodge Russia from the control of North Manchuria, the Chinese Government in Manchuria continued to pursue, with the aid of the Nationalists, the ambitious policy of getting rid of the Japanese in Manchuria. At this time Japan should have made a decision to check this dangerous plan.

The Minseitō Government tried to avert the would-be outcome of the Chinese advance into Manchuria by means of a conciliatory policy towards China, the same policy which it had formerly pursued. Even within the scope of this "friendship" policy, Baron Shidehara should have been able to plan something more constructive and effective in view of the possibility of an ultimate crisis. As a matter of fact, however, the leaders of the Minseitō Government had very different views on this matter and adopted a series of domestic and international policies in order to deal with the situation then prevailing. Internally, they adopted a drastic deflation policy by returning to the gold standard at the old parity, as described in the preceding chapter. Internationally they made Japan a party to the London Naval Treaty of 1930 and refrained as much as possible from continental entanglement —a policy which was necessarily linked with the domestic financial policy. But the fate of this policy showed all too clearly that it was serving a lost cause and only inviting a more reactionary external policy.

On October 7, 1929, the British Government, through the Secretary for Foreign Affairs, Arthur Henderson, invited Japan to participate in the Naval Limitation Conference to be held in January 1930. The Japanese press generally welcomed this move, reflecting the prevalent public feeling about the post-War system of collective security. Immediately upon the receipt of the British note, a Cabinet meeting was held on October 8, when it was decided that an affirmative reply to London should be drafted under the joint supervision of the Prime Minister, Foreign Minister and Navy Minister. The Cabinet was naturally anxious to obtain unanimous support by government circles, both civil and military, of the announced demands of the Navy, including a " seventy per cent ratio ", on which much stress was laid.

While the Navy Department was studying the British note, Premier Hamaguchi, in an address before the Minseitō convention at Nagoya on October 13, made the first public utterance of the Government on this subject. He stated that the basic policy of Japan at the coming Conference would be threefold: (1) her Navy should constitute no menace towards others, while at the same time she would tolerate no threat of insecurity from others; (2) the aim of the Conference should be an actual reduction in naval armaments; (3) Japan would be willing to accept a ratio lower than that of either Great Britain or the United States provided that it would be adequate for defence in any contingency. This broad outline of policy for the Conference was favourably received by the press. Meanwhile the draft reply prepared by the Foreign Office was carefully scrutinized at a joint conference of high officers of both the Foreign Office and the Navy Department, and was accepted. It was further approved by Reijirō Wakatsuki, the principal delegate, and finally accepted by the Cabinet. Foreign Minister Baron Shidehara stated that, though the wording of the draft was abstract, concrete proposals would be presented in preliminary negotiations and that the Government was prepared to press the policy thus decided upon. The text of the reply to the British Government was made public on October 18.

The concrete proposals to be presented to the Conference were drafted by the Navy Department. When completed, the draft was submitted to a joint conference of the Navy

Department and the Foreign Office. Having been approved by this conference, it was submitted to the deliberation of the Cabinet, which formally approved it on November 26, and after obtaining the Imperial sanction, the final instructions were given to the delegation on the same day. The instructions, though secret, were reported to contain the following three fundamental demands as the essentials of the naval policy of Japan: (1) a 70 per cent ratio *vis-à-vis* the United States in 10,000 ton, 8 inch gun cruisers; (2) a 70 per cent ratio *vis-à-vis* the United States in gross tonnage for all auxiliary craft; (3) not only opposition to radical reduction or abolition of submarines, but maintenance of the total of 78,500 tons, the tonnage being no less than that of either Great Britain or the United States.

In London, however, despite such thorough and deliberate preparations in which all parties concerned had cooperated, the Japanese delegation were obliged to accept the compromise of a 10:6 ratio in heavy cruisers, compensated for by slightly higher ratios in light cruisers and destroyers and equality in submarines. This compromise was reported to have been reached between the Japanese Ambassador, Tsuneo Matsudaira, and Senator Reed of the American delegation without any advice having been sought from the Japanese technical staff. It was even reported that Admiral Takarabe, the chief Navy delegate, was not fully consulted at all stages of these informal negotiations between Matsudaira and Reed, and yet, being unable to assume responsibility for the collapse of the Conference which might have followed his refusal, Admiral Takarabe was forced to assent to the compromise against both his personal wish and that of the technical staff.

The nature and extent of the compromise, however, became a vexed question between the Foreign Office and the Navy Department in Japan. The Foreign Office seemed to regard the compromise as legal—not as a mere proposal on the part of the American delegation, but as an agreement reached between the delegates of Japan and of the United States— whereas the naval authorities maintained that it was merely another American proposal, subject to further negotiations. Accordingly the Naval Staff issued the so-called " Admiralty Statement " on March 17, and Admiral K. Katō of the Naval Staff formally called on the Premier to explain the opinion of the Navy. This situation resulted in a conflict of opinions with respect to the fresh instructions to be dispatched to London. In the circumstances, the Foreign Office had to draw up draft instructions, embodying in principle the compromise arrived at London, independent of the Navy draft. In order to bring the Conference to a successful close, Premier Hamaguchi decided finally to adopt the Foreign Office plan in preference to that of the Admiralty. After an important meeting of the Big Three of the Admiralty, a Cabinet meeting was convened to adopt the Premier's plan regarding the final instructions. The Prime Minister explained that, in reaching his decision, he had taken into careful consideration the importance of fostering international peace, the nation's economic and financial situation, and the needs of national defence.

At first, the press and the public were united in supporting the stand of the Navy during the entire Conference, because they believed in the necessity and oppositeness of the three fundamental demands in so far as national defence and security were concerned. Since, however, a compromising attitude was adopted by the Cabinet, the press changed its tone to support the Cabinet in the interest of the Conference. But it should be noted that such a change was merely an evidence of the absence of a conception of a consistent international policy; it clearly reflected the lack of general knowledge of international relations in Japan at that time.

The Hamaguchi Cabinet adopted the compromise mainly because the domestic affairs which had compelled the Cabinet to pursue a certain set of financial and economic policies also called for an international accord on the naval question. That the Government desired a tranquil international situation was clearly indicated by Baron Shidehara when he stated that the Government expected the moral influence which the Treaty would exert upon international relations. It was clear, therefore, that this policy of the Cabinet presumed somewhat lasting peace which would ensue. The real issue over the matter, then, should have been a critical analysis of this presumption. Actually, however, the question of the London Naval Treaty became a totally different issue, resulting as it did in a complicated constitutional crisis which threw the public into utter confusion. The adamant and uncompromising stand of the Admiralty was reflected in the parliamentary interpellations of the opposition party and the attitude of some of the influential members of the Privy Council. The criticism of the Cabinet by the opposition party was, as usual, directed against the procedure which the Cabinet had adopted in the conclusion of the Treaty rather than against the substance of the Treaty itself. They charged the Government with having determined the nation's defence programme in utter disregard of the view of the Naval Staff, and declared that such an action constituted a violation of constitutional procedure. The Cabinet replied, in both Houses of Parliament, that the responsibility of the Cabinet for the conclusion of the Treaty was clearly constitutional because it had been carried out under the treaty-making power of the Throne upon the responsible advice of the Cabinet. The action of the Cabinet was constitutional as far as the concluding of the Treaty was concerned, but the real issue lay in the extra-legal process of determining a policy regarding naval strength, or that of determining the instructions to be given regarding such a policy. Unfortunately, in this process there was not perfect agreement between the Cabinet and the Naval Staff, an agreement which was absolutely necessary at least from the political point of view. Admiral K. Katō, the Vice-Chief of the Naval Staff, reiterated that the action of the Cabinet constituted an infringement upon the powers of his office, since it had been accomplished without the concurrence of the Naval Staff.

In spite of the stern opposition of the Naval Staff—both the Vice-Chief of the Naval Staff and the Vice-Minister of the Navy Department resigned—the Cabinet carried the matter to the stage of ratification. The Treaty was formally referred to the Privy Council on July 24, 1930. Instantly a sub-committee for inquiry into the Treaty was formed, and the delicate issue of the instructions was subjected to searching scrutiny. The committee requested that the Cabinet submit all the necessary data concerning the new naval replenishment programme and its bearing upon public finance. But the Cabinet refused to do so on the ground that the Treaty should be ratified before such documents and data were published. At one time the committee seemed to be stalled in its deliberations, and it looked as though it had devolved upon the Government to prepare for the worst development of the situation. Suddenly and mysteriously, however, the committee changed its attitude and unanimously decided to recommend the unconditional ratification of the Treaty. On October 1 the Privy Council, at its plenary session with the Emperor in attendance, approved unanimously the sub-committee's recommendation of the ratification of the Treaty without any reservation.

This victory for the Minseitō Cabinet, however, was bought at a very high price, too high, as was subsequently proved, for the leaders of the Cabinet. It was clear that the victory was attributable to their firm determination, especially on the part of Premier Hamaguchi, to carry out an international policy favouring harmonious relations with the United States and Great Britain even at the cost of overriding the wishes of the naval authorities and precipitating an internal constitutional crisis. Almost no one foresaw at that time that this crisis eventually would lead to a reign of violence culminating finally in the assassination of some of the leaders and the ultimate downfall of the Cabinet.

CHAPTER VI

THE MANCHURIAN INCIDENT AND ITS INTERNAL REPERCUSSIONS IN JAPAN

The Cause and Effects of the Manchurian Incident

Long before the Manchurian Incident, a serious situation had loomed in Manchuria which, as mentioned in previous chapters, should not have been overlooked by the responsible statesmen and the general public in Japan. The Government, however, was preoccupied with the London Naval Limitation Treaty as well as with the domestic troubles caused by its financial and economic policy. And the people at large were so bewildered and distressed by domestic affairs that they paid little attention to the situation on the Asiatic mainland.

After the spring of 1931 the gravity of the Manchurian situation had been aggravated by a succession of minor but complicated incidents. Fighting broke out in a rice-field of Wanpaoshan between Chinese and Korean farmers and the police of both sides in July. This was followed by widespread anti-Chinese riots in Korea and, in turn, by a revival of the anti-Japanese boycott in China. Late in June a Japanese officer on an intelligence mission in central Manchuria, Captain Nakamura, and his companions were detained, and later secretly killed by Chinese soldiers. The news of this came as a shock to the Japanese public and stimulated the growing demand for an immediate and decisive settlement of the whole complex issue, even if by force. As the Lytton Commission declared:

" In the course of September public sentiment regarding Chinese questions, with the Nakamura case as the focal point, became very strong. Time and again the opinion was expressed that the policy of leaving so many issues in Manchuria unsettled had caused the Chinese authorities to make light of Japan. Settlement of all pending issues, if necessary by force, became a popular slogan. Reference was freely made in the press to a decision to resort to armed force, to conferences between the Ministry of War, the General Staff and other authorities for the discussion of a plan with this object, to definite instructions regarding the execution, in case of necessity, of that plan to the Commander-in-Chief of the Kwantung Army, and to Colonel Doihara, Resident Officer at Mukden, who had been summoned to Tokyo early in September and who was quoted by the press as the advocate of a solution of all pending issues, if necessary by force, and as soon as possible. The reports of the press regarding the sentiments expressed by these circles and some other groups point to a growing and dangerous tension." (The Report of the Commission, Chap. III, Sect. 7.)

However, these so-called " cases " or " affairs " were only superficial manifestations of the broader issue, that is, the fundamental conflict of policy between Japan and China. One aspect of this conflict was the railway problem. The Japanese Foreign Office, headed by Baron Shidehara, approached this problem as a necessary step towards a conciliatory settlement of the whole Manchurian problem. The South Manchuria Railway particularly was in difficulties because of the competition of the Chinese-owned railroads. The rates on the Japanese railroads were quoted in gold, and the sudden rise in the value of gold currency after Japan's return to the gold standard in January 1930 caused customers to prefer the Chinese railroads on which fares were paid in relatively cheap silver. In addition to this difference in railway fares, the Chinese tariff and construction policies were clearly intended to compete with the Japanese railroads.

The policy to be adopted by Japan in the proposed negotiation regarding the railroad problem, as outlined by Baron

Shidehara in the Diet on March 9, 1931, was considered both practical and conciliatory. It was based on the assumption that this problem should be, and could be, settled amicably by reaching a compromise on technical and management questions. It included the following important items : (1) the reference of the pending construction of railroads by Japan to further conferences ; (2) the settlement of the problem of competitive and parallel lines by some technical and management arrangements ; (3) the discussion of the question of railroad transportation and tariff rates with a view to arriving at a workable agreement ; and (4) the adjustment of Japanese rights and Chinese obligations on railroads constructed by Japanese capital. This programme was reported to have been proposed without any previous consultation with the military authorities who had been jealously watching the situation in Manchuria.

No matter how " weak " the policy might have been, had the negotiation based on the above points been successful in winning the assent of the other party, Baron Shidehara would have won the Japanese public to his side, and his mistake in ignoring the military authorities would not have been a fatal blow to his position. As it was, however, the negotiations were hindered from the outset by the attitude of the representatives of Chang Hsueh-liang. The main reason for the failure of the negotiations was political, for the Chang Government was controlled by the Kuomintang Government which demanded that Chang transfer the right of diplomatic negotiation with Japan to Nanking, a demand which was tantamount to a refusal to negotiate. The leaders of the Nanking Government and their followers misjudged the future of Sino-Japanese relations so badly that they refused to believe either in Baron Shidehara's sincerity in proposing the conference or in the advantage of settling the Manchurian problem with the most moderate and conciliatory Foreign Office ever to exist in Japan. They also failed utterly to take into account the probable effect on the Japanese mind of the failure of Shidehara's last attempt at peaceable negotiation and its inevitable reaction upon Japanese policy in Manchuria.

The news of the failure of the railroad negotiation was a signal for the outbreak of the various minor incidents described in the early part of this chapter. During the summer of 1931 the Japanese people, both in Manchuria and at home, began to feel increasingly uneasy and irritated over the growing disorder in Manchuria. On August 4, they heard for the first time a responsible official freely allude to a coming disaster, when General Minami, the Minister of War, spoke publicly on the Manchurian situation at the annual meeting of the Commanders of Divisions. In that speech, covering the whole field of politics, diplomacy and national defence, he foreshadowed the determined stand of the military authorities towards the Manchurian situation. This unusual address by the War Minister created a great sensation among Cabinet circles as well as the general public. It was accepted as a public notice to the nation that the military was now united in demanding a more vigorous policy in Manchuria and that it was determined to take the situation into its own hands and to seek solution in its own way. It was on September 18 that the memorable incident occurred at Mukden.

The news of the explosion of a bomb on the track of the South Manchuria Railway at Liutiaohu Station north of Mukden and of the attack by Japanese troops on the Chinese military barracks at Mukden reached Tokyo early in the morning of September 19. Within a few hours the Japanese troops had seized a half-dozen strategic points, occupied the Mukden area, including the arsenal and barracks, and disarmed Chinese troops. An extraordinary meeting of the Cabinet was called at 10:30 a. m. to deliberate upon the policy of the Government towards the grave situation in Manchuria. At this meeting War Minister Minami made a detailed report on the causes and progress of the conflict. Baron Shidehara, the Foreign Minister, insisted that the military operations should be confined within the narrowest limits compatible with the circumstances. After the meeting, the Prime Minister announced that the Government had decided on a policy of " non-aggravation" and that instructions in accordance with this policy, had already been sent to the Commander-in-Chief of the Kwantung Army through the War Minister.

Contrary to the passive and abstract attitude of the civilian members of the Cabinet at the outset of the Incident, the policy of the military was active and concrete. According to the statement of the Army issued to the press on the afternoon of September 20, it was understood: (1) that additional detachments would be sent to Manchuria if counter-attacks were attempted by Chinese troops; (2) that it would be for the Cabinet to decide whether solution of all outstanding issues over Manchuria and Mongolia should be sought in connection with this Incident—in the view of the Army, however, this opportunity should be taken to seek such a solution and this view would be conveyed to the Cabinet through the War Minister; (3) that these issues should be dealt with as local issues, and not by negotiation between Nanking and Tokyo; and (4) that non-aggravation of the situation was desirable, but that did not necessarily mean the restriction of military operations, and this latter point was to be made clear to the Government.

Within five months after the beginning of the Incident, the Japanese troops drove out all Chinese garrisons, seized all strategic points in Manchuria, and occupied Mukden, Changchun, Chinchow, Harbin and other Manchurian cities. The main Chinese forces were withdrawn within the Great Wall by the end of 1931, and the opposition which the Japanese continued to meet in different parts of Manchuria was of only an irregular nature. By August 1932 the remnants of the original Northeastern armies were to be found only in the remote parts of the provinces of Kirin and Heilungkiang. Meanwhile the new state of Manchoukuo was established on March 1, 1932, and the normal conditions were gradually restored under the guidance of the new administration in cooperation with the Japanese military authorities.

The Effect of the Incident on Domestic Affairs

The Manchurian Incident was a momentous event which had a tremendous and far-reaching effect on the domestic affairs of Japan. Despite the fact that a few of the intelligentsia and a group of persons of communistic tendencies were skeptical or even opposed to the venture, the vast majority of the people gave emotional support to this military activity on the continent. The firm determination of the Army together with the necessity for military operations meant a shift of political leadership from the political parties to the military organization. The people's dissatisfaction with the corrupt practices of the parties as well as with their passive and inert foreign policy in the face of the revolutionary changes in the Far East was clearly reflected in the popular expectation that something satisfactory might emanate from the untried policies of the military camp. Such a psychological factor was accompanied by another vague, yet deep-rooted dissatisfaction, namely, the discontent with the existing order, which the world-wide economic crisis and depression had created among the people. Even the intelligentsia, believing in the communist theory of the collapse of capitalistic society, embraced the idea that a " planned-economy " of any kind was the only way out of the existing situation.

It may sound strange and even unreasonable to the democratic mind of the West to expect industrial reconstruction by
a military organization whose function is limited to the field
of national defence.   But such superficial observation would
fail to grasp the real nature of the socio-political organization
of Japan.   The spirit of regimentation and the technique of
organization, which are needed to a considerable extent for
efficient administration today, were entirely neglected in Japanese party politics where the parties, with a view to furthering
their own interests, were interested only in manipulating the
administrative machinery which they had received from the
bureaucrats.   Moreover, after fifteen years of party government, the time had come for some neutral elements having no
connection with the parties to renovate the demoralized and
corrupt political scene.   The military was hailed by the people,
not because of its tested skill in administration, but rather because of the integrity it had maintained by virtue of its independence from party politics.

These underlying conditions should be taken into consideration in observing the repercussions of the Manchurian Incident
upon the internal affairs of Japan.   The initiative was taken
by the Army both in aiding the establishment of the new state
of Manchoukuo and in revitalizing the administrative organizations of Japan in Manchuria.   The economic programmes
pointing towards state socialism appealed to the people as
a means of eliminating private exploitation and capitalistic
profiteering.   Despite its implications in international relations, especially regarding the accepted principle of the Open
Door in China, and despite the difficulties in obtaining sufficient
capital and materials for the industrial development of Manchuria, this determined policy was received somewhat uncriti-
cally by the general public.   In later years, perhaps the policy

was to be criticized on its merits or modified in the light of its results, but the position of the military in the country's politics after the Manchurian Incident hardly could have been challenged.

Thus leadership in politics was shifted to the military. While the liberals were urging caution and prudence in handling the Manchurian affair in view of its international implications, the more impatient groups were gradually gaining influence with the public. The Seiyūkai did not fail to take every opportunity to discredit the China policy of the Minseitō Cabinet and to exert all its influence to bring about its downfall. Even certain members of the Minseitō began to voice opposition to its own Government's policy. Thus, on November 21, Kenzō Adachi, Home Minister and a leading member of the Minseitō, issued a public statement to the press, openly advocating a " national Government " in view of the delicate nature of international relations. The difference of opinion which ensued between opposing factions within the party finally led to the downfall of the Cabinet on December 11, 1931. Tsuyoshi Inukai, President of the Seiyūkai, formed a new Cabinet two days later, with Lieutenant-General Araki as Minister of War, and took over the conduct of the nation's affairs.

The general election of February 1932, which followed the dissolution of the Diet, returned an overwhelming Seiyūkai majority. It did not, however, arouse much popular interest because it was fought mainly on the domestic issue of financial policy, viz., " deflation or reflation ", with both of the major parties evading the issue of foreign policy. After a few months the Seiyūkai Cabinet came to an end with the May 15 Incident, in which Premier Inukai and other prominent persons were assassinated. The public was stricken with revolutionary atmosphere. Cool-headed people deplored, of course, this act of a band of fanatical young officers and radical youths deeply interested in rural reform. It must be admitted, however, that, reckless and over-enthusiastic though it was, their programme for political reform met with some public sympathy. At this time a national Government headed by Admiral Viscount Saitō was organized with the heavy responsibility of coping with the turbulent situation. Under this Cabinet recognition of Manchoukuo and withdrawal from the League of Nations became a possible if not an inevitable consequence.

CHAPTER VII

THE SYSTEM OF COLLECTIVE SECURITY VERSUS JAPAN'S CONTINENTAL POLICY

The Withdrawal from the League of Nations

The first official statement concerning the view of the government on the situation was announced on September 22, 1931, three days after news of the outbreak of the Manchurian Incident had reached Tokyo. It explained that military action was necessary to prevent an imminent danger to Japanese interests in Manchuria, and that Japan harboured no territorial ambition in the region, and broadly intimated that she would insist to the end upon direct negotiation with China. It made clear also that Kenkichi Yoshizawa, the Japanese Ambassador to France, had been instructed to notify the Council of the League of Nations which was to meet on September 25 that Tokyo intended to withdraw the Japanese troops to the railway zone as soon as the situation improved.

Such a gesture of assurance was, however, nothing but the expression of a vain hope of the Foreign Office, vain because the actual power of directing the nation's foreign policy was fast shifting from the Foreign Office to the military. While the news of the bombardment of Chinchow was disturbing the Foreign Office and causing alarm in Geneva, the Council, at a request from China, reassembled on October 13. At this stage, acting under instructions from Tokyo, the Japanese representative pointed out the importance of knowing the historical background of the Incident and tried to convince the Council that the League should not attempt any form of intervention by merely adhering to the letter of the Covenant, but that a solution should be sought on the basis of the penetrating understanding of the actual situation.   The Council, however, approved the President's resolution calling for the complete withdrawal of Japanese troops to the railway zone before the next Council meeting, set for November 16, and adopted it by 13 votes to 1.

Meanwhile the Foreign Office was preparing the "basic five points" for the solution of the Sino-Japanese conflict, to serve as the basis for direct negotiations between the two countries.   These principles were made public by the Cabinet on October 25 and constituted the swan song of Shidehara diplomacy.   I personally think that it was the most constructive and yet conciliatory formula ever produced by the Foreign Office.   But it was too late to be effective; it should have been made public and proposed to China before the Manchurian Incident.

Along with the formation, on December 13, of a new Seiyūkai Cabinet, Japanese activities in Manchuria took a new turn as a result of the renewed activities of the Chinese Northeastern armies.   The new developments gave the United States an opportunity of intervening in Far Eastern affairs. On January 7, Secretary of State Stimson addressed identical notes to Tokyo and Nanking, enunciating what came to be known as the "Stimson Doctrine" of non-recognition.   It declared:

> "In view of the present situation and of its own rights and obligations therein, the American Government deems it to be its duty to notify both the Imperial Japanese Government and the Government of the Chinese Republic that it can not admit the legality of any situation *de facto* nor does it intend to recognize any treaty or agreement entered into between two Governments, or agents thereof, which may impair the treaty rights of the United States or

its citizens in China, including those which relate to the sovereignty, the independence, or the territorial and administrative integrity of the Republic of China, or to the international policy relative to China, commonly known as the open-door policy, and that it does not intend to recognize any situation, treaty, or agreement which may be brought about by means contrary to the covenants and obligations of the Pact of Paris of August 27, 1928, to which Treaty both China and Japan, as well as the United States, are parties."

In its reply to Washington on January 16, 1932, the Japanese Government stated in part that, contrary to the view advocating the application of the Nine-Power Treaty, "the present unsettled and distracted state of China" had not been contemplated by the parties at Washington in 1922, and that consequently "it may in material respects modify their [the Washington treaties] application, since they must necessarily be applied with reference to the state of facts as they exist". The same attitude was taken by the Japanese Government towards the resolution of the Assembly of the League of Nations adopted on March 11, in connection with the development of the incident around Shanghai, wherein it had unanimously agreed that the provisions of the Covenant were entirely applicable to the dispute, thereby rejecting the Japanese argument emphasizing the "special character" of Manchuria which had been indicated in the Japanese reply to the Stimson note.

In spite of the protests of the nations of the world interested in the system of collective security, the new continental policy of Japan progressed steadily towards recognition of the establishment of Manchoukuo. The new state of Manchoukuo was formally founded on March 1, 1932, and on March 9 the former Emperor Hsuan Tung, now known as Henry Pu Yi, was inaugurated as regent of the new state in its capital at Changchun. On March 12 the new state issued a notice by cable to various foreign powers, informing them of the establishment of Manchoukuo and requesting them to recognize it.

For Japan naturally the most important problem was how she should deal with the new regime in Manchuria. Sooner or later, she had to recognize the new state; otherwise she would be unable to cooperate openly with it. In view of the international situation, however, the Inukai Cabinet decided to postpone *de jure* recognition pending further developments in the new regime. Later on, with the fall of the Inukai Cabinet, public demand for immediate recognition became pronounced and was vigorously expressed in the Diet. Upon the arrival of the Lytton Commission in Tokyo on July 4 after several months of study in Manchuria and China, the demand for recognition grew. Count Uchida, the Foreign Minister, made it plain to the members of the party that Japan intended to accord recognition at an early date. Finally, on September 15, Japan signed the protocol. The logical conclusion of this act was Japan's withdrawal from the League of Nations. The unacceptability to Japan of the report of the Lytton Commission, together with its proposals for the solution of the Sino-Japanese conflict had already been made known to the Commission while it was in Japan conferring with the Government. When the League Council commenced its long awaited consideration of the Lytton report on November 21, the Japanese representative, Yōsuke Matsuoka, in an address before the Council expressed a dissenting view, elaborating the crucial points which had been expounded already in the official observations of the Japanese Government. He went on to declare that any suggestion for settlement which the League of Nations might decide to make must be governed by three principles: namely (1) the terms must be such as could be effectively put into operation and would achieve and preserve peace in the Far East; (2) a solution must be found for the disorder in China ; and (3) the League of Nations must assume responsibility for the execution of any plan for settlement which it recommended.

On December 15 the Committee of Nineteen of the Assembly adopted the report of its sub-committee, accepting the Lytton recommendation that neither the restoration of the *status quo ante* nor the maintenance of Manchoukuo was satisfactory. When the Committee of Nineteen consequently reached an impasse in its deliberations, it issued a communique stating that efforts at conciliation had failed and that it would now proceed to draft a report under Article XV, clause 4, of the Covenant of the League of Nations. While the proceedings at Geneva were thus moving towards a hopeless impasse, Viscount Saitō, the Prime Minister, and Count Uchida, the Foreign Minister, defended Japan's Manchurian policy and argued before the Diet that "any plan for erecting an edifice of peace in the Far East should be based upon the recognition that the constructive force of Japan is the mainstay of tranquility in this part of the world ".

On February 24, 1933, the Assembly of the League of Nations adopted the report of its Committee of Nineteen, censuring the Japanese action in Manchuria and recommending the policy of non-recognition of Manchoukuo. Thereupon the Japanese delegates withdrew from the Assembly room, and on March 27, a formal notice of the Japanese intention to withdraw from the League was announced to the world.

The Significance of the Manchoukuoan Empire in Japan's Continental Policy

On the occasion of the celebration of the second anniversary of the new state, it was announced that Manchoukuo was to be an empire, the Chief Executive, Henry Pu Yi, was to be enthroned, and some parts of the provisional constitution revised.   Several official statements declared that this decision did not represent in any sense a restoration of the Ch'ing Dynasty.   The reasons which prompted the change in the political structure of the state, however, were not only inadequately explained, but, in the author's view, not clearly understood even by the Japanese people.   It was indeed solemnly declared that the enthronement and the establishment of an empire was intended to promote the development of the spirit of the creation of Manchoukuo, *Wang Tao* (the Kingly Way), and also that it was a proof of popular confidence in the new emperor.   But whether the people understood its real significance in terms of world politics as well as of Japanese internal politics is open to doubt.   As a matter of fact, the entire Japanese people welcomed the establishment of the empire as a powerful argument for the improvement and progress of Manchoukuo, but they evidently did not fully appreciate the political significance of the new commitment.   It seems, therefore, important to make clear the underlying causes of the change and to enquire into its possible effects on the political history of the world as well as on that of the Far East.

Internally, Manchoukuo, which is not an empire in the accepted sense of that term, cannot be said to have possessed all the necessary elements of statehood.   First among the deficiencies was the ambiguous position of the chief executive in the provisional constitution.   Moreover, his position was inconsistent with the political philosophy of *Wang Tao*, which demands that a ruler shall be more than merely the highest administrative organ of the state.   Then, too, there were and still are the problems of nationality and of territorial jurisdiction.   As to the former, the Declaration of Independence of Manchoukuo states that the five racial or ethnic groups constitute, on an equal basis, the original members of the new nation.   However, there has not yet been any law of nationality whereby the status of the peoples in Manchoukuo is defined. Finally, the problem of territorial sovereignty, the third necessary element of statehood, has yet to be completely solved.

Thus, as far as the elements of statehood are concerned, Manchoukuo is to be regarded rather as a virtual protectorate of Japan than as an independent state in the modern sense. As long as the military agreement between Manchoukuo and Japan and Japanese predominance in government personnel continue to exist, Manchoukuo as a state cannot properly be said to exist. These imperfections in the national status of Manchoukuo are clearly understood by the Japanese, who justify them on the grounds that the foundation of the new state was a sudden outcome of the Sino-Japanese conflict, and that many years of constructive work are required before statehood in the modern sense of that term can be fully attained. So the Japanese have determined to pour their energies and wealth into this enterprise, giving aid in various forms and directions. The policy of making Manchoukuo an empire was clearly intended to solve at least one of the problems of statehood mentioned above. At the same time it will in no small measure facilitate solution of the others.

Nevertheless, this policy should not be regarded simply as a means of solving such problems alone. The forces which brought it about must also be analysed. There seem to have been three kinds of influences at work. In the first place, the movement for the restoration of the Ch'ing Dynasty, supported by the minor, but influential, Manchu group in the Manchoukuo Government, was partly responsible, although the enthronement was avowedly not brought about in order to meet this demand. Apart from their selfish motives, the Manchu group might justly claim that the restoration would be fitting, at least in appearance, because the Ch'ing Dynasty had once ruled over other racial groups under one imperial system. But this reasoning is not only in contradiction to the spirit of the foundation of Manchoukuo, because the constituent ethnic groups of the state were declared to be on an equal status, but also it has no real connection with the destiny of Manchoukuo as conceived by the Japanese. The aspirations of the Manchus are common knowledge, but they are neither shared nor supported by the Japanese. It may be said, therefore, that although the restoration movement may have been a powerful influence in making for the establishment of an empire, it was an influence which had to be modified in various ways so as to meet the needs of the existing situation. Evidence of that modification lies in the repeated official statements that the old emperor and the new, although personally identical, are politically distinct.

The second influence responsible for the establishment of the empire was the Pan-Asiatic movement. This movement is not yet organized with any coherent programme under a prominent leader. But there are many small groups of so-called Pan-Asianists loosely affiliated through study organizations and other connections. The political ideas adopted and the policies advocated by these groups have leaned towards traditionalism, agrarianism and totalitarian nationalism in conformity with fascist tendencies, as against the rationalism, capitalism and individualistic liberalism imported from the Western democratic countries.

This Pan-Asiatic movement is divided into two sections according to the economic policy advocated for Japan. The right-wing section, with no particular interest in economics, inclines to advocate continuation of the present policy almost in its present *laissez-faire* form, while the left-wing would revise it from the more or less totalitarian point of view. In spite of this difference, it must be noted that there is general agreement among the Pan-Asianists regarding the establishment of a monarchical system in Manchuria as a practical expediency to meet the hostile attitude of China and the unfavourable policies of the Western nations.   Further, it should be noted that they entertain a peculiar interpretation of the nature of the social institutions of Asia.   They consider that the traditional and historical socio-cultural elements of the Asiatic community would be a suitable basis for racial co-ordination in line with their policy of Pan-Asianism, and that such would constitute an ideal state for the Asiatic peoples at large.   To them the monarchical system in Manchoukuo commends itself, not only as an edifice of loyalty attractive to their abstract, unanalytical, subjective minds, typical of the Orient, but also because it is regarded as promoting such political aspiration.

It is surely evident, however, that this interpretation of the needs and possibilities of the Asiatic community is narrrowly limited in its application to actual world affairs.   An industrialized Japan, which alone can support the growing population, does need the Asiatic mainland, but it also needs the world markets.   Indeed, the large expenditure for the Manchurian expedition and the economic development of Manchoukuo may be said to have been met mainly by the economic gains from Japan's export trade which expanded widely all over the world.   If the Pan-Asianists should pursue their course of action regardless of this fact, they would not only be inviting the political hostility of the West, with which they must deal, but also economic exclusion by it, with which they cannot deal.   This is generally realized by enlightened leaders in both Manchoukuo and Japan.   The Pan-Asiatic influence, like the restoration influence, may have made for the empire, but clearly it was not strong enough to produce quite the sort of empire it envisaged.

The last but not the least important influence which brought about the establishment of the empire was one which emanated from official circles in Japan as well as in Manchou-kuo. These officials are practical-minded people, long accustomed to making adjustments here and there in a compromising spirit. They have acquired extensive knowledge of constitutional problems, from their practical experiences with the political transformation of Japan. They consider that the system of constitutional monarchy in Japan furnishes an example of the success of a monarchical system with an Asiatic people and that the Japanese experience of its functioning can be valuable in directing the policy of a new state similarly constituted. It is probably this influence—this wholesome, practical influence—that was strongest in establishing a monarchical Manchoukuo, and in giving that monarchy its present form. The traditional respect for the name and the historic sense of loyalty has been to a certain extent satisfied by the person of the monarch himself and by the political philosophy associated with the monarchy, and have been utilized to sustain the monarchical movement. But it must be remembered that the establishment of the empire has been essentially a practical experiment.

The establishment of an empire in Manchuria has also an international aspect. From the standpoint of Japan as well as Manchoukuo, it was intended as an evidence of the consolidation of the new state. It is, however, only a pious hope that this constitutional change will cause other countries to reverse their non-recognition policy. Although some aspects of recent developments in Manchoukuo are encouraging, the policy of non-recognition sponsored by the United States and the League of Nations is not concerned primarily with observations of the internal conditions of the new state, but rather with the necessity, to their way of thinking, for the maintenance of the international treaties and peace machineries which have been established in the past fifteen years.

If at some future time a change should become evident in the policy of non-recognition of Manchoukuo by other countries, it will be due, not to any change in the internal conditions of Manchoukuo, but to a changed outlook on international relations in China or to a new attitude of the world at large with regard to the maintenance of international peace. It must be admitted that the system of collective security of the post-War period has partially, if not wholly, broken down since the Manchurian Incident of September 1931. The Japanese people believe that since their withdrawal from the League of Nations, the functioning of peace machinery within that framework, at least in the Far East, has become almost impossible. In such circumstances any international cooperation which excludes Japan as the stabilizing force in East Asia and as an influential force in achieving international peace would be a new source of disturbance not only in that region but in the whole world.

PART TWO

A NEW ORDER IN EAST ASIA AND JAPAN'S FOREIGN POLICY

CHAPTER VIII

JAPAN'S CHINA POLICY AFTER THE MANCHURIAN INCIDENT

From the Manchurian Incident till the Tangku Truce

It was perhaps inevitable for Japan's foreign policy after the Manchurian Incident to promote the founding of Manchoukuo, then to recognize this new state formally, and ultimately to withdraw from the League of Nations. Throughout that period, the Kwantung Army in Manchuria was mopping up the defeated and scattered Chinese forces in order to ensure the position of the new state against an attempt at "recovering the lost provinces" by the Nanking Government and the North-eastern armies under Chang Hsueh-liang. The last major operations were to wipe out the anti-Japanese and anti-Manchoukuo forces in Jehol — a campaign which the Japanese Army commenced on February 18, 1933, and concluded by swiftly reaching the Great Wall after the fall of the capital on March 4.

The next step was to conclude a truce with a view to stabilizing the relations between Manchoukuo and the North China provinces. Considerable importance was attached in Japan to the possibility of such a truce because it might not only be made a test of whether the conflict could be settled by negotiations on the spot, but might also prove an opportunity of resuming the normal relation between Tokyo and Nanking. The military authorities were awaiting a suitable opportunity for the truce and the Foreign Office was making preparations for the eventuality of diplomatic conferences with the Chinese Government. On the part of China, Chang Hsueh-liang assumed the responsibility for the loss of Jehol and went abroad. His place was filled by General Ho Ying-chin, Minister of War in the Nanking Government, who was made the responsible head of the Peiping branch of the National Military Council. Later the Peiping Political Readjustment Council was established with General Huang Fu, former Foreign Minister at Nanking, as its head. Thus the direct control of the Nanking Government was extended as far as the Great Wall and various measures to strengthen the defence of North China were carried out. The result was that the Kwantung Army and the troops under the direct command of Nanking came face to face — a dangerous situation which presently led to a clash between the two forces. The Kwantung Army grasped the first chance offered, advanced beyond the Great Wall into Hopei, and approached dangerously near Peiping and Tientsin. Thereupon on May 31, the expected truce was finally concluded at Tangku. The terms were as follows :

1) The Chinese Army shall immediately withdraw to the regions west and south of the line from Yenching to Changping, Kaoliying, Sunyi, Tungchow, Hsiangho, Paoti, Lintingkow, Nangho and Lutai and undertakes not to advance beyond that line and to avoid any provocation of hostilities.

2) The Japanese Army may at any time use aeroplanes or other means to verify carrying out of the above article. The Chinese authorities shall afford them protection and facilities for such purpose.

3) The Japanese Army, after ascertaining the withdrawal of the Chinese Army to the line stated in Article I, undertakes not to cross the said line and not to continue to attack the Chinese troops and shall voluntarily withdraw to the Great Wall.

4) In the regions to the south of the Great Wall and to the north and east of the line as defined in Article I, the maintenance of peace and order shall be undertaken by the Chinese police force.

The said police force shall not be constituted by armed units hostile to Japanese feelings.

5) The present agreement shall come into effect upon its signature.

Taking advantage of this Tangku Truce, efforts were made by the Japanese authorities to restore communications between Manchoukuo and China. Public opinion in China was naturally antagonistic to such plans, but since General Chiang Kai-shek was too much occupied with the anti-Communist campaign and the settlement of the Southwest problem to lead personally a national movement against Japan, Wang Ching-wei was appointed president of the Executive Yuan and made responsible for dealing with the Japanese problem. Wang Ching-wei's policy was " partly resistance, partly negotiation ", but being well aware of the difficulty of resistance, he instructed Huang Fu to carry on negotiations with Japan. Agreements were thus effected governing the establishment of customs offices near the Great Wall (June 3), through railway traffic between Peiping and Shenyang (July 1), and through postal transmission (January 1, 1935). Of course there was a limit to the accomplishments of the two-year " regime " of Huang Fu and a number of outstanding issues in the demilitarized zone had to be left unsettled.

On the whole, however, it looked as though the strained Sino-Japanese relations were steadily returning to normalcy, and a *ballon d'essai* was raised on both sides seeking for an opportunity of effecting a wholesale readjustment. Thus, Kōki Hirota, Foreign Minister in the Okada Cabinet, who succeeded Count Uchida known for his " scorched earth " diplomacy, spoke as follows before the Diet on January 23, 1935. His tone was moderate and created a favourable impression in China.

"I fervently hope not only that China will soon recover her stability, but that she will awake to the realization of the whole situation of East Asia and undertake to meet the genuine aspirations of our country. In view of our position as China's neighbour and a stabilizing force in East Asia, it is our policy to try to assist China in the attainment of this goal. I may add that the Japanese Government are glad to acknowledge the fact that, as has been indicated in the gradual solution of various long pending questions, there is today a growing trend among the Chinese people to appreciate the true motive of Japan. I hope that China will collaborate with us further in that direction. "

Responding to this "conciliatory diplomacy" of Hirota, General Chiang Kai-shek published in the press of February 2 a statement regarding Sino-Japanese rapprochement which read in part :

"Since it can be discerned that the Japanese Foreign Minister spoke from the bottom of his heart, the whole Chinese nation, both governmental leaders and people alike, must try to appreciate all that he meant.

. . . That both sides should mutually speak and act in good faith in accordance with the principle of equality is, to my mind, the only means for going forward on the road towards a bright future . . . .

It is highly essential, therefore, for the improvement of relations between the two countries that the anti-Japanese sentiment which, on our part, has been entertained in the past and the sense of superiority on the part of Japan should be rectified at the same time."

Nature and Limits of Sino-Japanese Rapprochement

There were two focal points in the diplomatic relations between Japan and China during the first half of 1935. The first was the new political situation created in North China after the Tangku Truce. The old North-Eastern armies and other feudalistic forces which had been a source of constant disturbance in Manchoukuo were wiped out, and the central authority of the Nanking Government was made to fill the vacancy. Now the question was how the Peiping Political Council, the embodiment of this central authority, would fulfil its intended role of serving as a buffer between the two countries, and how the policy of " partly resistance, partly negotiation " would work. The second focal point was the atmosphere in Tokyo and Nanking which had seemed to be more and more suitable for direct negotiations between the two Governments.

These two aspects of Sino-Japanese relations were delicately interdependent although superficially they appeared even contradictory, because one was an attempt to settle specific questions of essentially local import while the other represented an endeavour to achieve an all-round readjustment of Sino-Japanese relations by orthodox diplomatic means. In the opinion of the Japanese Government, they were not necessarily contradictory, and accordingly efforts were made to attain two objectives, viz., disappearance of anti-Japanese agitation throughout China and realization of economic cooperation in North China. Minister Ariyoshi was instructed to negotiate with the Nanking Government to this end. Huang Fu in North China, on his part, while agreeing with the Nanking Government that a political understanding should precede whatever might be achieved in the economic sphere, was doing his best in the light of the Japanese wishes to act as intermediary between Nanking and the Japanese authorities in North China with a view to bringing about Sino-Japanese cooperation in economic enterprises. (One result was the establishment of the China Development Company in November 1936.)

These negotiations between the two countries were not without results. First, the Nanking Government, in accordance with a resolution of the National Political Council, circulated instructions to the provincial and municipal branches of the Kuomintang to suppress anti-Japanese agitations and boycotts. At that time an explanatory note by the Secretary of the Central Executive Committee of the Kuomintang was attached to the circular to make it clear that this policy of General Chiang Kai-shek and Wang Ching-wei was completely in accord with the wishes of the Central Kuomintang Council. Secondly, Dr. Wang Chung-hui, formerly President of the Judicial Yuan, visited Japan en route to the Hague in April-May 1935, and at about the same time several other prominent Chinese also came to Japan with a view to promoting commerce between the two countries. As a result of conversations then carried out, the Sino-Japanese Trade Association was established both in Tokyo and Shanghai in January 1936. Thirdly, the Japanese Government paid a compliment to China by elevating the status of its diplomatic mission, and both countries came to exchange ambassadors from June 14, 1935, onward. Fourthly, a few pending questions of minor importance, such as those of radio communications and the clearance of debts between the two countries, were settled.

However, these efforts to improve diplomatic relations were doomed to fail, for in the latter half of the year the fundamental difference, which had existed all the time underneath, began to crop up on the surface, and the situation in North China markedly deteriorated. Before describing it in the following chapters, it may be well to recall that the Hirota policy at that stage followed a certain formula which may be summed up as follows :

1) China must abandon her anti-Japanese policy and that of playing off one foreign country against another or of relying upon the Western powers to check the influence of Japan ;

2) China must respect the fact of the existence of Man-

choukuo and definitely give up the attempt to recover her lost provinces ;

3) Japan and China must jointly devise effective measures for preventing the spread of communism.

CHAPTER IX

SINO-JAPANESE RELATIONS OVER THE NORTH CHINA PROBLEM

So-called Ho-Umetsu Agreement

The stability brought about by the Tangku Truce was only temporary. The advance of the direct control by Nanking into North China aggravated rather than alleviated frictions. The assassination of two Chinese journalists in Tientsin, destruction of electrical lines, and other disquieting events took place in succession in the early summer of 1935. The Japanese military authorities who had been watching the situation with growing concern now concluded that the conciliatory policy of Nanking as exemplified in the suppression of anti-Japanese movements was insincere, and in May 1935 they presented a series of demands to both Peiping and Nanking, the terms of which were as follows :

1) Dismissal of General Yu Hsueh-chuug, Chairman of Hopei, and withdrawal of the 51st Army and the 2nd and 25th Divisions from Hopei.

2) Dissolution of various anti-Japanese organizations and punishment of those responsible;
   a) dissolution of the Third Regiment of the Military Police and dismissal of its head, Chiang Hsiao-hsien;
   b) closing of the local branches of the Kuomintang;
   c) dissolution of the Political Training Corp of the Peiping Military Council and dismissal of its head, Tseng Fuang-ching;
   d) suppression of the Fu-hsing Club, known as the "Blue Shirts" and similar secret organizations and the C. C.

3) Punishment of those responsible for the assassination case (dismissal of Mayor Chang of Tientsin, etc.).

The Chinese reply stated in brief:

1) Tientsin will be set apart from Hopei and made a special municipality under the direct control of Nanking; and special care shall be taken to promote friendly relations with Japan.

2) The Mayor of Tientsin as the responsible official for the assassination case, will be dismissed and Wang Keh-min, acting Chairman of the Peiping Political Readjustment Council, will be appointed Mayor to deal with the situation.

3) New corps for the purpose of peace preservation will be established and Shang Chen appointed Commander.

4) The Government of Hopei will be transferred to Paoting.

Thus the Chinese reply ignored practically all of the crucial points. At the same time the Nanking Government approached Foreign Minister Hirota, requesting that the question be settled through mediation. Since, however, the Japanese Foreign Office and the Army had agreed that the matter should be handled directly by the local military authorities, Foreign Minister Hirota merely noted the Chinese request, while the War Office in Tokyo immediately instructed the General Staff of the North China Garrison to negotiate with the Chinese authorities. This collaboration between the Foreign Office and the War Office served to dispel the rumour then prevailing that they were at variance on some aspects of the question. The Nanking Government, now realizing the importance of the situation, was obliged to conclude that the only way to settle the question was to do it on the spot.

General Ho Ying-chin, the Chinese representative, referred to Nanking for instructions. Although there were some strong objections in the Nanking Government, Wang Ching-wei, Huang Fu and Ho agreed, and Chiang Kai-shek approved, their decision to accept the Japanese demands *in toto*. This reply was transmitted by Ho to the Japanese authorities on June 10. This is what is generally called the "Ho-Umetsu

Agreement ", although, as a matter of fact, there does not exist any such formal document signed by the two generals as the name suggests. At that time, the following principles were reportedly agreed to as well : (1) measures were to be taken to prevent further aggravation of the situation ; (2) wide power was to be given to the authorities in North China to deal with Sino-Japanese questions ; (3) the personnel of various organizations in that region was to be such as would promote cooperation. On the same day, in accordance with the agreement, the " Goodwill Mandate " was promulgated, forbidding any one to "indulge in discriminatory or provocative speeches or acts ".

At about the same time, the detention by the Chinese authorities at Changpei, Chahar, of a group of Japanese officers led to negotiations between General Chin Te-chun, head of a bureau in the Chahar Government, and Major-General Doihara, Chief of the Kwantung Army's Special Service Section. A settlement which has become known as the Chin-Doihara agreement was brought about on July 27. Its main provisions were reportedly as follows : (1) dismissal of General Sung Che-yuan from his post as Chairman of Chahar and withdrawal of his 29th Route Army from the neighbouring area of Manchoukuo ; (2) dissolution of Kuomintang organizations in Chahar.

The Appearance of Autonomous Regimes in North China

Changes which were made in accordance with the " Ho-Umetsu agreement ", and changes indirectly resulting from it, were both significant and far-reaching. At one stroke, General Yu Hsueh-chung with his 51st Army and all divisions under the central Government were driven out of Hopei. All Kuomintang organs in the province were suppressed. The Peiping Political Readjustment Council was dissolved on August 28, and the Peiping Branch Military Council abolished on November 26. The personnel of officials was changed. The area of the demilitarized zone was enlarged.

It now seemed that an impetus had been given the threatening situation which had existed in North China since the summer months of 1935. Presently a series of autonomous movements broke out. In early November, rumours were frequently heard of a scheme to establish an autonomous regime in five provinces of North China—Hopei, Shantung, Shansi, Chahar and Suiyuan. The central figures were General Sung Che-yuan, formerly chairman of Chahar, now Garrison Commander of the Peiping-Tientsin area—a position which he had held since August 28—, General Han Fu-chu, Governor of Shantung and General Shang Chen, Governor of Hopei. While nothing came out of it, towards the end of November schemes on a much smaller scale materialized in two regions, one distinctly anti-Nanking and the other under at least the nominal control of Nanking. The former, the East Hopei Autonomous Council, was the first to apperar ; it was inaguurated at Tung-chow on November 25, with Yin Ju-keng, administrative commissioner for the demilitarized zone in East Hopei, as Chairman. It was to control the whole of the demilitarized zone together with four semi-demilitarized *hsiens* (Hsiangho, Paoti, Changping, Ningo) neighbouring on the west, and consisted of eight other members most of whom were commanders in the Peace Preservation Corps. It declared its independence of the National Government, proclaimed its autonomous and anti-communist nature, and to control the whole of the national, provincial or *hsien* revenues.

On the following day (November 26) the Nanking Government sent General Ho Ying-chin to Peiping as representative of the Executive Yuan there—a post which he did not after all assume—and appointed General Sung Che-yuan Pacification

Commissioner for Hopei and Chahar provinces in addition to his post as Garrison Commander of Peiping and Tientsin. Out of the negotiations carried out between these generals and the Japanese officials emerged the Hopei-Chahar Political Council. On December 12 the Nanking Government formally appointed General Sung Che-yuan to the chairmanship of the Council together with 16 other Council members. And with this Chairman his 29th Route Army was also installed in this region.

The emergence of these two regimes was interpreted both in China and abroad as indicating that Japan was planning to introduce into North China the same ideology as had been embodied in the establishment of Manchoukuo ; in particular, the oft-quoted " Tada Statement " issued on September 24, 1935, was generally regarded as shedding much light upon the real intentions of the Japanese Army.

Against this Japanese offensive, the Nanking Government was stiffening its attitude. It not only stood in the way of the Japanese attempt to settle the North China question through the medium of the Hopei-Chahar Political Council, but tried to undermine the pro-Japanese group within the Council by secretly increasing the influence of the Kuomintang. Its constant objective was the restoration to North China of the *status quo ante*, or the " centralizing " of North China.

In such circumstances, the position of the Hopei-Chahar Political Council was naturally a very difficult one. The Japanese Government also found it difficult to find a formula by which to adjust the specific question of the Army's demand regarding North China to the general question of Sino-Japanese diplomatic relations as a whole. Its formula seems to have been the restriction as far as North China was concerned, of the scope of negotiations with the Nanking Government—in other words, recognition of the Nanking Government " as the central Government of China within a specified area ". Clearly this was incompatible with the Chinese demand for the centralization of diplomatic power in Nanking.

Foreign Minister Hirota, however, modified and elaborated his skeleton three principles on the strength of a Chinese view that China might accept a proposal for economic cooperation which would not involve the question of sovereignty, and worked out the following principal subjects for diplomatic negotiation with Nanking: (1) the anti-Japanese policy should be abandoned, and Japan and China should jointly promote economic cooperation between them; (2) Japan, China and Manchoukuo should live together politically and economically in North China, and China should do her best that she should ultimately be able to recognize Manchoukuo; (3) Japan, China and Manchoukuo should cooperate in defending North China and Mongolia against the spread of communism. These are Hirota's " three principles " as officially proclaimed and were formally approved at a Cabinet meeting of October 8, 1935.

The reply which the Nanking Government made, in response to the above " principles ", through General Chiang Tso-pin, its Ambassador to Japan, before he left Tokyo in November, seems to have been: (1) China would strictly control anti-Japanese agitation and movements in accordance with the " Goodwill Mandate " and promote Sino-Japanese economic cooperation as best as she could; (2) China would agree to the proposal for common defence by China and Japan of North China and Mongolia from the threat of communism; (3) China would recognize the special position of North China provided that it does not impair the sovereignty and administrative integrity of China; indicating thus that China was willing to cooperate with Japan but would not accept any situation which would ultimately result in her fomal recognition of Manchoukuo.

Later, in view of the development of the autonomous movements in North China, the Nanking Government presented to the Japanese Government the following six items intended for the settlement of the North China problem:

1) China would cooperate with Japan in preventing the spread of communism;

2) As far as its application to North China is concerned, the new monetary system would be subjected to appropriate modification;

3) In view of the close relationship between the peoples of North China and Manchuria, China would help to smooth the economic relations between China, Manchuria and Japan;

4) Appropriate power to control public finance would be given to the Hopei-Chahar Political Council;

5) The same Council should also be given the power to bring about local and reasonable settlement of outstanding international issues;

6) China would ensure that the administration of the same Council were based on the wishes of the people, that able men were recruited, and that ideal rule were practised.

On the surface at least, this proposal undoubtedly seemed reasonable, but the Japanese military authorities in North China were so strongly imbued with a sense of distrust of Nanking's sincerity that they demanded the inclusion of another item recalling for the removal of the central armies from Hopei. This the Chinese refused to accept and unfortunately no negotiations were undertaken upon the basis suggested. Thus the situation went from bad to worse. In short, Japan and China failed to come to any agreement or understanding over the North China questions, including the autonomy movement and the status of the East-Hopei Autonomous Government; both parties, felt thoroughly dissatisfied with the existing situation, but did little to improve it.

In the meantime, before the year ended, Wang Ching-wei, concurrently Prime Minister and Foreign Minister, had been shot and wounded at Nanking (November 1). The ambitious plan for monetary reform had been successfully carried out with British help (November 3) and had considerably added to the prestige of Nanking. At the height of the student movement, Tang Yu-jen, Vice Foreign Minister and a prominent figure in the Wang Ching-wei group, had been assassinated at Shanghai (December 25). A thorough reorganization of the Cabinet had taken place and the pro-Western group had virtually eliminated Wang Ching-wei's following (December 7–12). Now Chiang Kai-shek was President of the Executive Yuan and General Chang Chun, Foreign Minister. In such changed circumstances, the possibility of Chinese foreign policy becoming sympathetic to Japan had become remoter than ever. In response, some people in Japan had come to demand a stronger and more determined policy vis-à-vis China, while others had begun, on the contrary, to advocate the advisability of " re-understanding " China. Amidst such a conflicting state of affairs, the general public had now become decidedly uneasy over the outlook of Japan's relations with her neighbour.

The Anti-Japanese Uprising in China and Subsequent Sino-Japanese Negotiations

The emergence of the Hopei-Chahar Political Council signified an advance in Japan's China policy. The Japanese attempt to secure peace and order in the neighbouring region of Manchoukuo by driving off antagonistic forces was the logical sequence of the policy of establishing that state. But at the same time it entailed a fundamental readjustment of relations with China—an extremely difficult problem which could not be settled unilaterally. There were ways in which to tackle the difficulty : either a policy of virtually ignoring Nanking and dealing directly with the Hopei-Chahar Political Council or one of attempting to normalize Sino-Japanese relations as a whole by direct negotiations between Tokyo and Nanking.

The former was a realistic policy advocated by the Army and supported by public opinion, and it tended to gain ground proportionately as the negotiations between the central Governments appeared more and more difficult. With the turn of the year, this tendency became more marked than ever. Just then the February 26 Incident brought on an unprecedented crisis in domestic politics, and although it was brought to a close without delay, one of its far-reaching results was inevitably a stronger North China policy.

On the other hand, the drive of the Nanking Government for internal unity had progressed steadily, and the atmosphere of antagonism towards Japan had become more widespread and stronger in all of China. Faced with this development the necessity of all inclusive diplomatic negotiations with Nanking was felt in Japan, especially among the group of people advocating, as mentioned already, the advisability of " re-understanding " China. In any case the task imposed upon the Foreign Office was a most delicate one, because it was expected to carry out an exceptionally strong policy by pacific means.

After the February 26 Incident, Foreign Minister Hirota became Prime Minister, and presently Hachiro Arita, Ambassador to Nanking, was called home to assume the Foreign Ministership, his place in China being filled by Shigeru Kawagoe, Consul-General in Tientsin. As was clear from this diplomatic " line-up ", the intention of the Foreign Office was to re-open negotiations under the banner of " conciliatory diplomacy " based on the " three principles ". The situation in China, however, had become unmistakably more critical and threatening, and irrespective of the wishes of the diplomatic authorities in both countries or in spite of the " Goodwill Mandate ", anti-Japanese incidents took place repeatedly throughout China, irritating the public in Japan. In particular, the killing or attacking of Japanese nationals at Chengtu (August 24, 1936), Pakhoi (September 3), Hankow (September 19) and Shanghai (September 23), threatened to be of grave consequence. Minor incidents occurred at Swatow (September 17), Taiyuan (October 26) and Fengtai (June-September).

Partly with reference to these incidents, partly with a view to settling the pending questions of long standing, the Japanese Government instructed Kawagoe, its new Ambassador to China, to re-open formal negotiations with the Nanking Government. The Ambassador left Shanghai for Nanking on September 13 and started conversations with Foreign Minister Chang Chun on the 15. His principal purpose was believed to be discussion of the North China problem. It was reported then that in accordance with the decision which had been reached jointly by the Foreign Office and the Army, he had been instructed to demand a " special " status for the whole of the five North China provinces on the ground of their being contiguous to Manchoukuo—whereas the original plan had been less ambitious, seeking to " specialize " Hopei and Chahar only. Japan was reportedly determined to take appropriate steps to attain her objective if the Nanking Government would not give a satisfactory answer.

The Chang-Kawagoe negotiations lasted till December 3, during which period eight successive conferences were held —all of them fruitless. In the course of these negotiations, at one stage (October 6) the Chief of the Far Eastern Bureau of the Foreign Office, K. Kuwashima, was sent to Nanking to convey new instructions to the Ambassador ; at another

(October 8) the latter was directly received by General Chiang Kai-shek; and on September 28 Foreign Minister Arita indicated Japan's determined stand in his statement to the foreign press in Tokyo which concluded as follows :

> " The outcome of the present negotiation can take only one of two courses; Sino-Japanese relations will be either very much better or very much worse. In the existing situation they shall not be permitted to drift in the ambiguous state of affairs as has been prevailing in the past. China is now at the momentous cross-road, to decide whether or not to shake hands with Japan. I very earnestly hope that China will grasp our hand in friendly response, whatever difficulties she may have to surmount."

One may well imagine what situation he was facing at that time.

When the fifth conference ended in November 21, it had been made clear that the greatest difficulty was still the North China problem. Consul-General Suma in Shanghai was then called home to present an interim report. Hsu Shih-ying, Chinese Ambassador in Tokyo also conversed with Foreign Minister Arita and was reported to have explained the Chinese position thus : the Nanking Government earnestly hoped, of course, that the negotiations would be successfully concluded as soon as possible, and this would be clear from the fact that more than one half of the Japanese demands had already been accepted; if, however, Japan's demands were such as would violate the territorial and administrative integrity of China, China could not but refuse them ; China therefore sincerely hoped that the Japanese Government would give the matter serious consideration and that both Governments would be able to deal with the difficult situation in a conciliatory and cooperative spirit. He thus implicitly indicated the wishes of the Nanking Government either that the Japanese demands on North China and the joint defence against communism be modified or that they be dealt with independently of the other items. Foreign Minister Arita, however, seems to have insisted upon the inseparability of all Japanese demands and to have urged that China should make every effort to accept them without placing too much stress on the formal aspect of sovereignty.

Meanwhile, in the middle of November news of the Suiyuan Incident leaked out. Despite the official denial of the Japanese Government, it was assumed that there was Japanese assistance behind the Inner Mongolian forces which had invaded Suiyuan, and a widespread patriotic and anti-Japanese agitation appeared throughout China. The Kuomintang through its Intelligence and Publicity Department stirred up national feeling in a way highly inimical to the continuation of the Sino-Japanese negotiations. It declared in part that the key to the negotiations was solely in the hands of Japan ; national indignation had now been so aroused by the invasion of the northern territory by large troops that the whole nation was watching it with far greater concern than the Sino-Japanese negotiations. Thus the negotiations were brought to a deadlock. They had been given up to all intents and purposes, when the eighth conference adjourned on December 2. That the whole series of conferences achieved very little, if anything, was palpable, for both sides did not even agree as to what had actually taken place in the course of the conversations. In contradiction of Kawagoe's statement of December 3 claiming that an agreement in principle had been reached on several specific questions, China disclosed, in a semi-official statement on December 1, the conditions or counter-proposals which she had presented on each of these questions, thus indicating that the agreement had not really been complete. The statement of the Japanese Foreign Office spokesman issued on December 10 and that of the Nanking Government published on the following day, both concerning the negotiations, were also contradictory.

A few days later the whole world was electrified by the news of the Sian Incident.

Sino-Japanese Relations after the Sian Incident

On December 12, 1936, at Sian General Chang Hsueh-liang suddenly attempted a coup and arrested General Chiang Kai-shek who had come to hold military conferences on the emergency situation in Suiyuan. For the moment, guesses circulated freely as to the latter's safety, but he returned safely to Nanking on December 25. Contrary to the fear entertained for a while, the unification of China advanced rather than deteriorated, and the position of the Nanking Government was strengthened rather than weakened. The protracted struggle which had hitherto been staged between the Government and the Communists now gave way to positive collaboration. China seemed to have been united in the common cause of resisting Japan.

The Third Plenary Session of Kuomintang met at Nanking on February 15-22 and decided upon policies to deal with the last phases of the Sian Incident. The session manifesto then adopted, in so far as it referred to China's foreign policy, was exclusively devoted to elucidation of her policy towards Japan. Among other things the manifesto declared that the Kuomintang saw no need for revising China's foreign policy; that the Government should exert its best efforts in executing the policy already laid down; that China's consistent objective was to achieve internal autonomy and to cooperate with other nations; if there was still hope for peace, China was willing to continue her efforts in working for the preliminary readjustment of Sino-Japanese relations on the basis of equality and mutual respect of each other's territorial integrity; and that prerequisite for such readjustment was to get rid of the " false " regimes and to recover integrity of sovereignty.

It is scarcely necessary to point out that this declaration clearly indicated China's intention not only to get rid of the East Hopei Anti-Communist Government, but to abolish even the Hopei-Chahar Political Council which she had once at least recognized. Palpably the North China problem still proved to be the most serious obstacle to whatever adjustment was to be expected of Sino-Japanese relations.

Such strengthening of China's anti-Japanese front on the basis of a Kuomintang-Communist rapprochement could not but be reflected in the internal politics of Japan. The retirement of the Hirota Cabinet must be attributed, in the final analysis, to the public disappointment with developments in China. The succeeding Hayashi Cabinet which started off without a Foreign Minister, was unable to decide upon any new effective policy towards China. In his review of foreign relations delivered in the Diet on February 15, 1937, General Hayashi, concurrently Premier and Foreign Minister, referred neither to Hirota's principles nor to the six demands which had featured the Chang-Kawagoe negotiations, but simply stated : " It is of urgent necessity at this juncture to cultivate cordial feelings between the two nations and to improve their relationship so that they may be brought to work in close cooperation for the peace and stability of East Asia. And for this purpose we must foster mutual appreciation and bring about closer contact not only between the two Governments but also between the two peoples, and achieve in a more concrete form cooperation and mutual assistance of the two countries." The visit in China on March 21 of the influential group representing the Sino-Japanese Trading Association was one attempt to secure the intended cooperation between the two countries. But since any real economic cooperation would have required a prior political understanding, the result of any such efforts by businessmen was naturally very limited, to say the least.

Naotake Satō, who accepted the Foreign Ministership (March 3) upon his return from France, where he had been Ambassador, made his first utterance in the House of Peers on March 8 when he answered an interpellation and indicated the importance of resuming Japan's China policy on the new basis of equality and conciliation. Among other things he said that he thought that the Sino-Japanese problems should be re-examined from a new angle. It was a platitude that negotiations between any two independent states should be conducted on the basis of equality, but it sometimes occurred that this platitude was overlooked and that one nation hesitated to recognize the equal relationship of another, or was inclined to think that it was in a superior position. This sometimes greatly hindered diplomacy. As to whether the relationship of equality was being maintained in the Sino-Japanese negotiations or in the relationship between the two peoples, he would like to leave it to members of Parliament to judge. He intended to re-examine that point and to re-approach the question from a new starting point. By this he did not, however, mean any startling departure, but only a mere commonplace. If, as China had complained, Japan had not recognized the equality of China, it would naturally have proved a great obstacle to the negotiations and, therefore, he would sincerely listen to what China had to say and reconsider the whole matter. And from Japan's standpoint, too, he would explain to China as fully as possible what Japan wanted, what Japan considered her interests, and if negotiations could be made possible on that new basis, he intended to re-open them. Would this attitude prove effective? How would it be accepted in China? He did not yet know. But, only if Japan would make up her mind to speak on that basis, he felt that subjects for negotiations might be altered in various ways and benefits of various kinds might be expected. Within the limits of not sacrificing Japan's vital interests, he intended to assume an attitude as conciliatory as possible. He was sure that the Government would agree with him.

This frank expression of view by the Foreign Minister produced considerable repercussions both in Parliament and in the public. In fact, he had to amplify his view and correct misunderstandings a few days later, in view of the fact that strong objections had been raised in various circles. True, the Foreign Minister was courageous and conscientious enough to express frankly what he felt confident was the fundamental question in Sino-Japanese relations, but he ignored public opinion in that he merely stated an abstract principle of diplomacy without studying carefully the past history of the negotiations. The state of mind of the people was not receptive to such a straightforward view nor were the circumstances such as would render it practicable. True, it was accepted favourably in some quarters, but the public as a whole tended to be rather opposed. This was also true of the Hayashi Cabinet itself in which opinion was divided, as became clear from the speech of the Foreign Minister.

On the other hand, in China the hostility to Japan was increasing, and Foreign Minister Satō's theory of orthodox diplomacy, as in the case of the Shidehara diplomacy, only produced an effect contrary to what its author had intended. China had by then advanced from the stage of " Internal Unity " to that of " Resist Japan and Save the Country " ; she was even in the mood for an actual offensive against Japan.

Specifically, it was reported that nothing short of the abrogation of the Shanghai Truce, abandonment or modification of the Tangku Truce, or dissolution of the East Hopei Anti-Communist Government would satisfy the general sentiment in China. Actually the Hopei-Chahar Political Council inclined more and more towards Nanking, and General Sung Che-yuan, who had once agreed with the Japanese authorities on the construction of the Tientsin-Shihchiachuang railways and the mining of the Lungyen iron mines, came to evade the issue and insist, instead, upon the dissolution of the East Hopei regime.

In this threatening and delicate situation, the Japanese Government still tried to force her policy of economic co-operation upon China, who insisted upon the importance of effecting a general political agreement before negotiating on any specific economic questions. Inasmuch as China's economic relations with Great Britain and other countries gradually became closer and helped to strengthen China's policy of resistance to Japan, Japan also found it necessary to attempt an Anglo-Japanese understanding as a means of preventing the deterioration of Sino-Japanese relations. But it was an attempt born almost of desperation and was not expected to break the deadlock.

Thus the complete failure of the Hayashi Cabinet both domestically and in its China policy led to the appearance of the Konoye Cabinet. Thereupon a new situation developed. It was to be, however, not the peaceable resumption of Sino-Japanese diplomacy which everybody had hoped for, but a full-fledged armed conflict between the two countries which was beyond any power of control, including that of the Cabinet itself.

CHAPTER X

THE SINO-JAPANESE CONFLICT AND
ITS DIPLOMATIC ASPECT

The Outbreak of the Sino-Japanese Conflict

Those who were at all informed concerning the conflict of policy between Japan and China over the North China problem and the deadlock in the Sino-Japanese negotiations received the news of the clash at Lukouchiao, outside Peiping shortly before midnight on July 7, 1937 with a feeling as if an inevitable, if not exactly an anticipated, event had occurred. Both the Government and the people instinctively sensed a grave situation. Sincerely eager to prevent an aggravation of the situation, yet resigning themselves to its inevitability, they immediately began preparing for a national mobilization. In a situation where intense diplomatic negotiations had lasted more than a year and yet had failed to achieve any result whatever, the outbreak of war must have been almost unavoidable. Even if it had been averted at that particular time, it would have occurred at some later time.

In May of the preceding year (1936) Japan had sent additional troops to North China. The military authorities at that time had maintained that the increase of the garrison was necessary in view of the threatening situation in North China and that it was intended to enable the garrison to fulfil its function, *viz.*, protecting the lives and property of the Japanese nationals in that region. China had lodged a formal protest through her Ambassador, Hsu Shih-ying, pointing out that (1) there would be no need for reinforcements, (2) the reinforcements would irritate the Chinese people, and (3) they would be contrary to Hirota's principles of non-menace and non-aggression. But Foreign Minister Arita had contended that the actual situation in North China necessitated the reinforcements and that they were legitimate because they were based upon the Tientsin Treaty. From then on, frequent skirmishes had taken place between the troops of the two countries and the situation had been such as might have developed into serious fighting even if the general atmosphere had not been aggravated. The military manœuvres of the Japanese troops, the immediate cause of the Lukouchiao fighting, were a typical case. There was a conflict of opinion as to the legality of such military manœuvres. The Japanese view as expressed by the Foreign Office spokesman was as follows :

" Under the provisions of Article IX of the Joint Note of the Allied Powers concerning the Boxer Rebellion, and paragraph IV of the Note exchanged between Japan and China concerning the Restoration of Tientsin, the Japanese troops garrisoned in North China have been accustomed to carrying on manœuvres without being subjected to any restriction as to locality or time. It is provided that with the exception of practice with loaded bullets no notice need be given for particular cases of manœuvres. However, as a matter of fact, in order to remove the anxiety of the local inhabitants, notice has been gratuitously served in advance, in the manœuvre in question, though it was not a practice with loaded guns.

It may be added that other Powers maintaining garrisons in China may, and are, in fact, used to holding similar manœuvres frequently.

1) The neighbourhood of Lungwangmiao, where troops were illegally fired upon, lies to the northside of Lukouchiao, and having but few houses, is best suited for military manœuvres. The autumn manœuvre of last year and many subsequent manœuvres, large and small, have been held there, so that the place has come to be regarded as if it were a regular practice field for our troops. Moreover, the river beach of the Yung-

ting above and below the Lukouchiao Bridge has been frequently used as the grounds for target practice with the high land to the west as a mark.

2) Our troops, with the impending Annual Inspection in view, had been practicing continuously day and night in the locality in question. . . .

Upon the outbreak of the Lukouchiao incident, the Japanese Government decided at an emergency Cabinet meeting on July 11 upon a " non-aggravation " policy and also upon necessary steps for sending troops to deal with any unexpected development of the situation.   At the same time, the Government issued the following statement :

"The Japanese troops garrisoned in North China have always maintained a calm and patient attitude towards anti-Japanese outbursts in North China. But unfortunately, on the night of July 7th, an inevitable clash occurred when Japanese troops were wantonly fired upon by soldiers of the 29th Army, which had been cooperating with our forces in maintaining peace and order in the region. As a consequence the atmosphere in the Peiping and Tientsin districts grew so tense that even the lives and property of Japanese nationals were endangered. However, the Japanese authorities made strenuous endeavours to localize the affair and prevent it from becoming further aggravated, and succeeded in persuading the 29th Army authorities to agree to a peaceful settlement.

Yet, on the night of July 10th, the 29th Army, in violation of the agreement, suddenly fired upon the Japanese troops, causing considerable casualties. Besides, China has since pushed warlike preparations by increasing its forces on the first lines by ordering the Chinese troops at Suiyuan to advance southward and also by ordering central Government troops to the front. China has not only failed to manifest any sincerity to seek a peaceful solution, but has gone the length of flatly rejecting all Japan's offers for an amicable settlement at Peiping. This leaves no room for doubt that the present incident has been brought about as the result of well-planned armed operations on the part of China against Japan. There is no need of dwelling on the vital importance to Japan and Manchoukuo of the maintenance of peace and order in North China. What is most urgently needed is that the Chinese not only apologize for the recent lawless actions and manifestations of antagonism and opposition to Japan, but give an adequate guarantee against a recurrence of such outrages in the future.

An important decision has been reached by the Japanese Government at today's Cabinet meeting to take all necessary measures for dispatching military forces to North China.

But, desirous as ever of preserving the peace of East Asia, the Japanese Government has not yet abandoned its hope for peaceful negotiations effecting non-aggravation of the situation, and its hope for prompt reconsideration on the part of China which may bring about an amicable solution. As regards the safeguarding of the rights and interests of the Powers in China, the Japanese Government is, of course, prepared to give full consideration."

This declaration clearly demonstrates that the Japanese Government's fundamental policy was one of non-aggravation and local settlement. It was the prevailing circumstances which were almost beyond anybody's control that rendered it unsuccessful. As a matter of fact, the Konoye Cabinet had before the outbreak of the incident intended to permit S. Kawagoe, the Ambassador, to re-open negotiations with Nanking on the basis of a new China policy which it had adopted at a Cabinet meeting on June 18. The guiding principle of that new policy had been to begin with settlement of local and specific questions and to attempt a fundamental readjustment by degrees. The Cabinet had intended to take a realistic and restrained attitude, avoiding as far as possible the occurrence of any new friction between the two countries, and, therefore, not immediately to take up Hirota's three principles as subjects for negotiation, but to concentrate upon more concrete, economic questions in North China. At the same time, it has been intending to effect a general improvement in Japanese diplomatic relations with all powers having interests in China. The immediate and greatest task had been, to overcome the rather bitter differences of opinion and ideology which had existed within the country since the February 26 Incident, and then attempt a fundamental settlement of the China problem. In view of such a situation, it was hardly conceivable that the Cabinet should have possessed, when the incident broke out, any other formula than that of a local settlement of the affair. Premier Konoye himself made this clear when he said in answer to an interpellation on July 28 in the extraordinary session of the Diet that after the North China Incident had been settled locally, Japan would launch upon a policy of fundamental readjustment of Sino-Japanese relations. It was rather China who had been inclined to be ambitious or uncompromising. She had insisted, so it was reported, on a political understanding as the prerequisite to any agreements, thus demanding the removal of the abnormal conditions in North China including the Hopei-Chahar Political Council, the East Hopei Anti-Communist Government, the Japanese garrison, etc.

At the same time, China did not seem to have anticipated exactly a large-scale armed conflict with Japan at that particular juncture, for she had called a conference at Kuling to decide upon measures for the economic and political reconstruction of the country. But no matter what were the real intentions of the government authorities, the two peoples had been prepared for the tragic struggle to come. At any rate the circumstances then were such that once a collision of armed forces had occurred, whether accidental or not, it would not have been possible for either side to give way.

On July 11, a provisional agreement for settlement of the incident was reached when the representatives of the 29th Route Army accepted the Japanese demands, including the punishment of the Chinese officers responsible for the Wanping-hsien Incident, withdrawal of the Chinese troops from Wanping-hsien and Lungwanguino, control of all anti-Japanese organizations, etc. Had this agreement been carried out promptly and with sincerity, the incident might have been settled temporarily at least, but since the withdrawal of troops or the punishment of responsible officers was apt to be delayed, the atmosphere did not easily subside and still more unexpected incidents threatened to occur. In particular, at a conference which had begun at Nanking on July 8 neither side showed any signs of conciliation, but simply exchanged protests and accusations. Especially fatal was the Nanking Government's attempt to prevent local settlement by the Hopei-Chahar Political Council. Faced with such a situation, the Japanese Government presented an important note on July 17 requesting that all provocations on the part of China cease immediately and that the authorities on the spot be allowed to carry out the agreement mentioned above without interference. Japan felt obliged at that time to demand the withdrawal of the Chinese troops outside of a certain area as an emergency measure to avoid recurrence of similar incidents. The counter-proposals put forward by China were : (1) that both Chinese and Japanese troops be withdrawn simultaneously; (2) that the whole affair be settled by regular diplomatic process ; (3) that any local settlement be subjected to approval by the Nanking Government. It was now unmistakable that the attitude of the Nanking Government was diametrically opposed to that of Japan, and it must be admitted that this uncompromisingly orthodox attitude in the emergency situation, where clearly a local, provisional settlement was required, was to a very large extent responsible for the aggravation of the whole situation.   It is to be noted further that even after the outbreak of armed conflict, the two Governments were not willing to abandon their respective policies to which they had persistently adhered, namely that of a special status of North China in the case of Japan and territorial integrity in that of China.   The address given by General Chiang Kai-shek at Kuling on July 7 was one of the most eloquent expositions of this Chinese attitude.   He said in part : " The safety of Lukouchiao is a problem involving the existence of the nation as a whole, and whether the incident can be amicably settled comes within the comprehension of the term, ' limit of endurance '.   If it finally reaches the stage where it will be impossible to avoid the inevitable, then we cannot do otherwise than to resist and to be prepared for the supreme sacrifice. . . . If we abandon as much as an inch of our territory to the invaders without attempting to defend it, then we shall be guilty of an unpardonable sin against our race."

Thus things went rapidly from bad to worse.   When the Japanese forces had wiped out the 29th Route Army from the Peiping-Tientsin district and commenced to advance southward towards Paoting across the River Yunting and northward in the direction of Chahar and Sansi, General Chiang chose to draw attention to Shanghai.   Immediately the Japanese Settlement was in imminent danger of being smothered before the overwhelming numbers of the central troops. With the outbreak of fighting in Shanghai, the nature of the conflict definitely changed—from the North China Incident to the China Incident.

When on August 14 Chinese planes recklessly dropped bombs on Shanghai, the situation became impossible.   On the following day the Japanese Government called an emergency Cabinet meeting and issued the following important statement :

"The Imperial Japanese Government, in its desire to secure permanent peace in East Asia, has always striven to promote friendship and cooperation between Japan and China. However, an atmosphere of hostility towards Japan has been created throughout China by anti-Japanese agitations used as an instrument by the Nanking Government to arouse public opinion and to enhance its own political power. The Chinese, over-confident of their national strength, contemptuous of our power, and also in league with the Communists, have assumed towards Japan an increasingly arrogant and insulting attitude. Herein lies the cause of all untoward events which have arisen repeatedly during recent years.

The present Incident is but the inevitable outcome of this situation. Dynamite had been ignited; the inevitable explosion merely happened to occur on the banks of the Yunting. The terrible Tungchow massacre is also traceable to the same cause. In South and Central China, Japanese lives and property have been so jeopardized that our people have been compelled to evacuate, abandoning everything they had acquired after years of incessant toil.

As has been frequently declared since the outbreak of the present Incident, the Japanese Government, exercising utmost patience and restraint, has steadfastly pursued a policy of non-aggravation of the situation, and has endeavoured to reach a settlement locally and in a peaceful manner. In the Peiping and Tientsin area, our Garrison, in the face of countless Chinese provocations and lawless actions, has done no more than was absolutely necessary to secure lines of communications and to protect Japanese nationals there.

On the other hand, our Government advised the Nanking Government to put an immediate stop to provocative acts and to refrain from obstructing the negotiations being conducted on the spot. The Nanking Government not only refused to follow our counsel, but proceeded towards the completion of war-like preparations against us.   In flagrant violation of solemn military agreements, the Chinese moved vast armies northward menacing our Garrison, and concentrated troops in and around Shanghai. Their provocative attitude became more clearly defined at Hankow.   Finally at Shanghai, the Chinese opened fire upon our Naval Headquarters and bombed our warships from the air.

In this manner the Chinese have insulted our Government, committed acts of unpardonable atrocity against our country, and gravely endangered the lives and property of our nationals throughout China.   They have finally exhausted the patience of the Japanese Government.   It has thus become imperative to take drastic measures in order to chastise the lawless Chinese troops and to impress upon the Nanking Government the necessity for reconsideration of its attitude towards Japan.

That matters should have come to this pass is deeply deplored by the Japanese Government which earnestly desires the maintenance of peace in the Orient and sincerely hopes for the attainment of common prosperity and public welfare in Japan and China.   The aim of the Japanese Government is none other than the realization of Sino-Japanese cooperation.   Its only desire is to eradicate the anti-foreign and anti-Japanese movement rampant in China, and to eliminate completely the fundamental causes of unfortunate incidents such as the present one, with a view to bringing about truly harmonious collaboration between Japan, Manchoukuo and China.

Needless to say, the Japanese Government harbours no territorial designs.   Its sole intention is to bring to reason the Nanking Government and the Kuomintang Party both of which have persistently incited anti-Japanese sentiments among the Chinese people.   The Japanese bear no ill-will towards the innocent Chinese masses.   In conclusion we hereby state that the Japanese Government will spare no efforts in safeguarding foreign rights and interests in China."

The Fall of Nanking and German Good Offices for Peace

On December 17, Nanking was occupied by Japanese forces.

With the fall of the capital of the Nationalist Government, the Sino-Japanese conflict which had for four months been fought along two lines, in North China and the Yangtze Valley, entered a new phase.

On December 14, the Chinese Provisional Government was inaugurated in Peiping. The significance of this fact was twofold. On the one hand, it disclosed the two political undercurrents of North China—one representing the intention of the Japanese Army to keep North China independent of Nanking as a special region contiguous to Manchoukuo, and the other that of those Chinese who had been opposed to the dictatorial government of the Kuomintang and to the " colonization " of North China. The new Government may be regarded as an attempt to merge the two and to build " North China for the North China people " on that basis. As far as these two forces were sufficiently strong, therefore, the emergence of the new Government was historically necessary and, to that extent, rational.

On the other hand, the Chinese Provisional Government was not only " regional " in the sense noted above, but it was also meant to be " provisional " in the literal sense of the word, until a central, permanent Government should be established, absorbing all parties and groups sharing the same views and aspirations, even including members of the Kuomintang. This was clearly indicated in the declaration issued by the Government to the effect that when in the future members of the Kuomintang offered their services, it would gladly accept them; that it had arisen for the time being, simply because it could not allow China to be torn to pieces; and that it promised to disperse when the politics of the country should have returned to normalcy.

It was generally anticipated in Japan that when Nanking fell some sort of opportunity might be offered for peace, but this was from the beginning a hope without any foundation. The Nationalist Government showed no signs of giving in. On the contrary, it scattered to Hankow, Chungking and other places and eagerly reconstructed its fighting front against Japan.

The Japanese Government held a series of important conferences in the beginning of the new year 1938 to deliberate upon possible peace terms, as may be conjectured from Foreign Minister Hirota's statement referred to below; but having come to the conclusion that there was absolutely no hope for peace, it duly requested the Emperor to call an Imperial Council on January 11, to determine the fundamental principles for prosecuting the China Affair, and on January 16 proclaimed the famous decision " not to deal with " the Nationalist Government of China.   Up to this point, at least from the Japanese point of view, the fighting had been no more than an effort to settle the Lukouchiao Incident by means of arms.   It was not only an undeclared " war ", but the diplomatic relationship of the two countries had not been severed, for the representatives of the Nationalist Government were still stationed in Tokyo.   But from that time on, it definitely developed into a regular, if still undeclared, war and both the Government and the people of Japan were now definitely prepared for warfare, however prolonged.   The statement of the Japanese Government issued on January 16 read as follows :

"Even after the capture of Nanking, the Japanese Government have till now continued to be patient with a view to affording a final opportunity to the Chinese Nationalist Government for a reconsideration of their attitude.   However, the Chinese Government, without appreciating the true intentions of Japan, blindly persist in their opposition against Japan, with no consideration either internally for the people in their miserable plight or externally for the peace and tranquillity of all East Asia.   Accordingly the Japanese Government will cease from henceforward to deal with that government, and they look forward to the establishment and growth of a new Chinese regime, harmonious co-ordination with which can really be counted upon. With such a regime they will fully cooperate for the adjustment of Sino-Japanese relations, and for the building up of a rejuvenated China. Needless to state, this involves no change in the policy adopted by the Japanese Government of respecting the territorial integrity and sovereignty of China as well as the rights and interests of other Powers in China.

Japan's responsibilities for the peace of East Asia are now even heavier than ever before.

It is the fervent hope of the Government that the people will put forth still greater efforts towards the accomplishment of this important task incumbent on the nation."

Thus the opportunity for peace which seemed to have offered itself after the fall of Nanking was definitely lost. On January 22 in the Diet, Foreign Minister Hirota disclosed the fact that there had been a peace talk when Dr. Trautmann, German Ambassador in China, offered his " good offices to act as an intermediary " for peace between Japan and China. In his review of foreign affairs, he said :

" Some time ago when the Japanese Government received a proffer of good offices by the German Government to act as an intermediary for bringing about direct negotiations between Japan and China, they proposed, with a view to affording the Nationalist Government a last opportunity for reconsideration, the following four points as the basic conditions for the solution of the Affair :

1) China to abandon her pro-Communist and anti-Japanese and anti-Manchoukuo policies and to collaborate with Japan and Manchoukuo in their anti-Comintern policy ;

2) Establishment of demilitarized zones in the necessary localities, and of a special regime for the said localities ;

3) Conclusion of an economic agreement between Japan, China and Manchoukuo ;

4) China to pay Japan the necessary indemnities.

These items summarized the minimum requirements which were considered absolutely indispensable by the Japanese Government. It was my earnest hope that the Nationalist Government would sue for peace on the basis of these fundamental conditions. However, that Government, blind to the larger interests of East Asia, and ignoring both our magnanimity and Germany's friendly intention, exhibited no readiness to ask frankly for peace, but only sought to delay the matter and ultimately failed to send a reply that could be regarded in any way as sincere. The Nationalist Government having thus wilfully thrown away the last chance placed at their disposal by the Japanese Government, it became clear that there would be no hope of ever arriving at a solution by waiting indefinitely for any reconsideration on the part of the Nationalist Government. It is because of these circumstances that the Japanese Government issued on the 16th of this month the statement that they would from thenceforward cease to deal with the Nationalist Government. As is made plain in that statement our Government now look forward to the establishment and the growth of a new Chinese regime capable of genuine cooperation with Japan, which it is their intention to assist in the building up of a new and rehabilitated China. I am fully convinced that this is the only way of realizing our ideal of securing the stability of East Asia through Sino-Japanese cooperation."

CHAPTER XI

THIRD POWERS IN THE CHINA AFFAIR AND JAPAN'S DIPLOMATIC ACTIVITIES

Soviet-Japanese Relations after the Manchurian Incident

At this point in this description of the China Affair, it may be profitable to examine international relations as they were affected directly or indirectly by the Far Eastern conflict and the development of Japan's foreign policy in this changing situation.

To begin with Soviet-Japanese relations, it is sufficiently clear that the Japanese policy of promoting the growth of Manchoukuo in that particular form was shaped by considerations of Soviet-Japanese rather than by that of Sino-Japanese relations. The U.S.S.R. maintained an attitude of non-intervention at the time of the Manchurian Incident and has, since the emergence of Manchoukuo, adopted a realistic policy of dealing with the new situation as a fact. Thus, while concentrating a large number of armed forces along the Soviet-Manchoukuo border line, she has gone as far as to negotiate directly with Manchoukuo, not with the Nanking Government, regarding her rights and interests in that country, although Japan has also invariably been made a party to such negotiations.

The first important subject for such Soviet-Japan-Manchoukuo negotiations was the problem of the transfer of the North Manchuria Railway. After one year and seven months, the negotiations were successfully concluded on January 23, 1935. According to the official announcement made by the Japanese Foreign Office on March 11, "The Agreement for the transfer of the North Manchuria Railway will come into effect with the formal signing thereof when simultaneously all the rights of the U.S.S.R. concerning the North Manchuria Railway (including the subsidiary enterprises and properties) will be ceded to the Government of Manchoukuo. In return, the Manchoukuo Government will undertake to pay a sum of ¥140,000,000, besides about ¥30,000,000, to be paid as discharge allowance of various kinds to the employees of Soviet nationality to be dismissed. Payment of approximately one-third of the sale price will be made in cash and spread over three years ". And it was arranged that the remaining two-thirds should be paid in three years for commodities produced or manufactured in Japan or Manchoukuo ; actually Manchoukuo should pay for commodities which the U.S.S.R. Trade Representation in Japan purchased from either subjects or corporations of Japan or of Manchoukuo. What proved the greatest obstacle in the course of negotiation was the question whether the Japanese Government should guarantee the payment by Manchoukuo—a question which was finally settled affirmatively with the result that Japan and the U.S.S.R. formally exchanged notes on March 23, the U.S.S.R. giving thereby a *de facto* recognition to Manchoukuo.

Another consequence was that, whereas Japan viewed this transaction as purely commercial, Soviet Russia seemed to have intended it as a counter-offer for a non-aggression pact, a formula characteristic of Soviet diplomacy at that time. Japan and Manchoukuo, however, were not prepared for such a political understanding, nor did they see any urgent necessity for it. In their view, if Japan and the U.S.S.R. were to attain really friendly relations, the Soviet-Manchoukuo border disputes and the question concerning Outer Mongolia should be settled first, and until that time they would not be in a position to reach an agreement of a general character.

With a view to readjusting Soviet-Japanese relations through settlement of these specific questions, Japan offered to negotiate on the question of fixing the border line. The U.S.S.R. made a counter proposal for finding means of settling border disputes. Finally, both sides agreed to commence negotiations on these two questions simultaneously in Moscow and Tokyo. However, failing to come to an agreement regarding the sections of the border line to be fixed, the negotiations soon reached a standstill.

Frontier incidents have recurrently taken place since this time including those at Halha, Mishan, Suifenho (1935), Chichanghou, Changlingtzu (1936), Kanchatzu (1937), Changkufeng (1938) and Nomonhan (1939). Of these the last two were the most serious, for the former threatened to lead to the outbreak of war between the two countries and the latter resulted in regular pitched battles between the two highly mechanized forces. The causes of this recurrence of conflicts lie not only in the unsettled boundary, but in the fact that both Japan and the U.S.S.R. are keeping large armed forces facing each other, and perhaps, fundamentally, that the world policies of both countries have become increasingly antagonistic, as exemplified in the China Affair and the Anti-Comintern Pact between Japan, Germany and Italy. If there had been no conflict of policy other than the minor ones over the border line, fisheries, trade, etc., the relations between both countries would have been sufficiently improved to lead to some general agreement.

One notable fact in support of this view is the problem of the Fisheries Convention—a treaty right of Japan of thirty years' standing, originating in the Portsmouth Treaty. Whenever disputes occurred over a revision or extension, it was almost invariably at a time when the general diplomatic relations had been strained for some reason or other. For instance, towards the end of 1937, it was because an Anti-Comintern Pact was reportedly being negotiated between Japan and Germany that the U.S.S.R. refused at the last moment to sign the draft agreement of November 1935, concerning the revision of the Convention, although the refusal was explained on the ground that internal arrangements had not been completed. Since that time, the Fisheries Convention has not been renewed, but merely prolonged on a temporary basis. Likewise, numerous Soviet acts against Japanese diplomatic establishments and commercial rights and interests, such as the difficulties inflicted upon the North Sakhalien Mining Company and the North Sakhalien Petroleum Company, interference with trade at Vladivostok, refusal to put visés on the passports of Japanese Embassy staff members, and pressure to close Japanese consulates at Novo-Sibirsk and Odessa have accounted for increasingly strained Soviet-Japanese relations.

The fundamental cause of the various frictions in Soviet-Japanese relations is to be sought in each country's relations with third powers, especially with China on the one hand and with Germany and Italy on the other. Both countries being contiguous to China, the China policies of Japan and of the U.S.S.R. are naturally affected by each other. The strong Japanese policy regarding the North China problem led not only to an increase in the Soviet forces in the Far East, but to a decidedly closer relationship between the U.S.S.R. and China—a relationship which was indicated first by the cooperation between the Kuomintang and the Communists on the occasion of the Sian Incident of December 1936 and then by the non-aggression pact together with the alleged secret military alliance between Nanking and Moscow after the outbreak of the China Affair. This closer tie and the Soviet assistance to China, in turn, affected adversely Soviet-Japanese relations, compelling Japan to prepare for the eventuality of fighting on two fronts.

In such circumstances the possibility of concluding a general agreement like a non-aggression treaty between Japan and the U.S.S.R. must be regarded as extremely slight. A proposal for a non-aggression treaty was made by the U.S.S.R. first in 1931–2, immediately after the outbreak of the Manchurian Incident and again on August 17, 1935 when Yurenev, Soviet Ambassador in Tokyo, proposed to Foreign Minister Hirota the desirability of a treaty between Japan, Manchoukuo and the U.S.S.R. regarding not only the fixture of the boundary, but also the settlement of questions and disputes near the boundary. As mentioned already, however, both Japan and Manchoukuo preferred to fix the boundary itself before settling any other questions.

The outbreak of war in Europe, however, brought about momentous changes in the Far East. The conclusion of the Soviet-German Non-Aggression Pact, which virtually put a temporary end to the Berlin-Rome-Tokyo Axis, has been partially responsible for an improvement in Soviet-Japanese relations. Especially after the settlement of the Nomonhan Incident, it was reported that a joint commission would be organized to deal with the boundary question.

The changed situation in the Far East is such at the moment that Japan and the U.S.S.R. may reasonably be expected to adjust their relations at least on immediate and specific questions, unless their world policies, especially their China policies, are pushed in a direction immediately dangerous to each other. As long as Soviet-German co-operation continues in the West, and as long as Japan's relations *vis-à-vis* Great Britain and the United States remain unadjusted, Japan's efforts will be directed towards the restoration and maintenance of friendly relations with the U.S.S.R.

The Anti-Comintern Pact

As the result of the Manchurian Incident, Japan was obliged to withdraw from the League of Nations in the face of the opposition of Great Britain, France and others whose foreign policies were supposedly based upon the principle of collective security. Japan thus became isolated, an isolation which was not only contrary to her traditional diplomacy, and contrary to national security, but which forced her, in consequence, to seek friends again among powerful nations outside the Anglo-American group.

Japan's foreign policy since the Meiji era had developed along the lines of maintenance of close relations with Great Britain and the United States, but since the World War her relations with these two powers have become increasingly less friendly. The Manchurian Incident especially delivered a severe blow to whatever hope remained of improving friendly relations. As a result, an anti-Anglo-American trend has assumed a conspicuous place in the politics of the country, while the influence of pro-Anglo-American groups has decidedly diminished.

At such a juncture the Hitler regime rose rapidly to ascendancy in Germany, with the avowed objective of correcting the "injustices" of the Versailles Treaties. It was perhaps natural, therefore, for both Japan and Germany to find a common ground upon which to draw closer to each other ideologically as well as politically, though in both countries there have existed elements which do not consider this tendency to be either advisable or advantageous. This is especially true of business circles, in view of the fact that their mutual relations have not been close enough and their interests in the Chinese market have been competitive. But beyond any such concrete considerations, the high politics and strategic policies of both countries tended to become mutually sympathetic on the minimum common basis of anti-communism.

Thus on November 25, 1936, the following " Agreement against the Communist International " was concluded :

" The Government of the German Reich and the Imperial Japanese Government, recognizing that the aim of the Communist International, known as the Comintern, is to disintegrate and subdue existing states by all the means at its command; convinced that the toleration of interference by the Communist International in the internal affairs of the nations not only endangers their internal peace and social well-being, but is also a menace to the peace of the world; desirous of cooperating in the defence against Communist subversive activities ; have agreed as follows :

Article   I

The High Contracting States agree to inform one another of the activities of the Communist International, to consult with one another on the necessary preventive measures, and to carry these through in close collaboration.

Article   II

The High Contracting Parties will jointly invite third states whose internal peace is threatened by the subversive activities of the Communist International to adopt defensive measures in the spirit of this agreement or take part in the present agreement.

Article   III

The German as well as the Japanese text of the present agreement is to be deemed the original text.   It comes into force on the day of signature and shall remain in force for a period of five years.   Before the expiry of this period the High Contracting Parties will come to an understanding over the further method of their cooperation."

At the same place (Berlin) on the same date both the Japanese and the German representatives signed a supplementary protocol providing for ways and means—including the setting up of a permanent committee—for putting the main agreement into practical effect.

Italy likewise became a signatory to the Pact on November 6, 1937.

These agreements created considerable repercussions in international relations and were generally viewed as an " axis bloc ". In other words, the combination was regarded as anti-democratic as well as anti-Comintern. As to the question which of these two characteristics was to play the greater role, the intentions of the three countries do not seem to have been necessarily the same. Even if they had agreed on this point, the Pact was not to remain unaffected by any changes which might occur in the world situation during its life.

The first result of the Anti-Comintern Pact was the recognition of Manchoukuo among other friendly steps taken by Germany and Italy—a development having an indirect bearing upon the Sino-Japanese conflict. The attitude of Germany was more complicated than that of Italy, as has been indicated by the friendly relations which she maintained with China ; but her moral support of Japan cannot be questioned. The Italian position has been more straightforward and strictly pro-Japanese. In particular at the Brussels Conference, Count Aldrovandi, the Italian representative, strongly supported Japan's case and maintained that the Sino-Japanese conflict was outside the scope of the Nine-Power Treaty.

The second result of the Pact was the conclusion of trade treaties. On July 5, 1938, the representatives of Japan, Manchoukuo and Italy signed " The Accord among the Governments of Italy, Japan and Manchoukuo for regulating the trade and the payment pertaining thereto between Italy on the one side and Japan and Manchoukuo on the other ". On September 14 the trade treaty which Germany had concluded with Manchoukuo on April 30, 1936, before her recognition of the latter was replaced by a new one of the same character.

Under its terms, Germany was to import Manchurian products to the amount of ¥163,000,000 annually and, in exchange,
to export German commodities worth ¥88,000,000 and pay
the remaining ¥75,000,000 in Reichsmarks. Furthermore both
countries mightimp ort, up to ¥10,000,000, goods for ordinary use other than the main products agreed upon.

Finally the "Berlin-Rome-Tokyo Axis" produced cultural
agreements as between Japan and Germany on November 25,
1938, and between Japan and Italy on March 25, 1939. The
German-Japanese cultural agreement is intended to bring
about "close collaboration" in the domain of science and
fine arts, music and literature, film and radio, youth movements and sports, etc., with a view to "deepening" the
relations between the two cultures "having their true foundations in the intrinsic Japanese spirit. . . and the German
national life" and "promoting the mutual knowledge and
understanding of both nations". The Italo-Japanese Agreement was meant to promote cultural relations by essentially
the same means.

Throughout 1938, Japan's relations with the United States
and Great Britain grew more and more strained because of
Anglo-American assistance to, and closer relations with China,
while Germany's position in Europe became increasingly
precarious in view of the so-called encirclement policy of
Great Britain and France after the Munich agreement. In
such circumstances, Japan, Germany, and Italy appeared to
be drawing closer than ever before, particularly since it was
freely rumoured during the summer of that year that secret
conversations were in progress with a view to changing the
ideological, economic or cultural combination into an outright
military alliance. The negotiations seem to have been continued until after Baron Hiranuma succeeded Prince Konoye
as Prime Minister in January, 1939. But in March 1939, the

German-Italian military alliance was concluded without Japanese adherence to it and finally in August, the sudden announcement of the Soviet-German Non-Aggression Pact violently upset the entire Axis relationship.

The Anti-Comintern Pact has now been terminated to all practical intents and purposes. This, however, does not signify any fundamental change either in Japan's policy against the Comintern or in the general relations between Japan and Germany. Although it appeared for the time being as though it had definitely ruled out the possibility of any close collaboration between Japan and Germany, it does not follow that it has impaired Japan's friendly relations with either Germany or Italy, since neither her fundamental policy in dealing with the China Affair nor her international position especially *vis-à-vis* the democratic powers is likely to change to any substantial extent.

Assistance to China by Great Britain, the U.S.A. and the League of Nations, and Japan's Policy

It is Great Britain and the United States in addition to the U.S.S.R. whose policies have of necessity a direct and decisive bearing upon Japan's position in the Far East, and as has been stated already, Japan's relations with these two foremost democratic powers have deteriorated markedly ever since the Manchurian Incident. Faced with a Far Eastern situation wherein Japan has launched an expansionist policy of her own, Great Britain and the United States have quickly discerned a serious danger not only to their rights and interests in that part of the world, but to the very foundations on which international security and order have been built. Consequently, they have adhered to a policy of checking the advance of Japan by rendering material as well as moral assistance to the anti-Japanese Kuomintang of China as a protection to their own Far Eastern interests, and in the name of the integrity of China and the sanctity of treaties.

It was in connection with the so-called Amau statement of April 19, 1934, that this conflict of policy between Japan and the Anglo-Saxon powers first appeared in a most glaring fashion. This much talked-about statement was the first, though not quite an official, announcement of Japan's China policy. It was a protest made because, after the League of Nations' mediation in the Manchurian Incident had broken down, some Western powers were openly selling armaments and helping the anti-Japanese policy of the Kuomintang under the guise of financial or technical assistance. The substance of the statement, which was practically the same as that of the instructions given by Foreign Minister Hirota to Japan's diplomatic missions to foreign countries, was basically a three-fold declaration : (1) Japan is solely responsible for the maintenance of peace and order in East Asia, and Japan has the mission, and determination, to assume this responsibility ; (2) China must ultimately depend upon her own re-awakening and efforts for her territorial and administrative integrity and the restoration of her internal order, and if China should attempt to play one foreign power against another in order to attain these objectives, Japan cannot help taking necessary measures to counteract this attempt ; (3) Any joint actions undertaken by foreign Powers, even in the name of financial or technical assistance, at this particular juncture after the Manchurian and Shanghai Incidents, would necessarily acquire political significance and lead either to the creation of " spheres of interest " in China or to an international control, or even partition of that country ; and, consequently, Japan cannot but strongly object to any such actions.

It is no wonder that this statement caused far-reaching repercussions in Great Britain and the United States and that both countries formally requested an explanation. The crux of the question was the bearing of such Japanese claims upon the principles of the Open Door and equal opportunity enunciated in the Nine-Power Treaty. But since Japan at that time had no intention, as Foreign Minister Hirota replied, of ignoring that Treaty, but only expressed what Japan had in mind, the whole matter would hardly be a subject for diplomatic negotiations. The negotiations were thus abandoned, but subsequently the British Foreign Secretary, Sir John Simon, indicated in the House of Commons on April 30 that the British Government would not agree that Japan alone could judge whether any action by foreign powers, such as the League of Nations' technical and financial assistance to China, would imperil peace and order. Secretary of State Hull of the United States also stated on the same day : " In the opinion of the American people and the American government, no nation can, without the assent of the other nations concerned, rightfully endeavour to make conclusive its will in situations where there are involved the rights, the obligations, and the legitimate interests of other sovereign states."

On the other hand, since the Manchurian Incident, Japan's attitude in dealing with situations in China affecting Sino-Japanese relations has tended to be increasingly realistic and political—so much so that it has created the impression that greater emphasis has been laid on political expedience than on considerations of treaty rights and obligations. This attitude has sometimes brought about situations where even the legitimate activities of third powers in China were virtually subjected to restrictions. This has been the case particularly since the outbreak of the present conflict. The Amau statement was an announcement of such a Japanese attitude and, in that sense, a highly significant event in Japanese diplomacy. Significant also has been the attitude of Great Britain and the United States of not recognizing any change resulting from the new Japanese policy, and of insisting that the existing treaty relations can only be altered with the assent of all parties concerned.

The diplomatic negotiations over the Amau statement were soon dropped, but in November 1934 Manchoukuo promulgated its oil monopoly law to become effective on April 10, 1935. This action seemed to offer grounds for the western fears aroused by the Amau statement, and the Governments of the United States, Great Britain and the Netherlands filed objections to this law. A similar case was the question of smuggling operations in North China—in the district under the East Hopei Autonomous Government—in the early part of 1936, when the British and American Governments made protests to Tokyo in May claiming an infringement cf the Open Door principle. The five-province autonomy movement in North China in the autumn of 1935 was another instance; in this case Great Britain and the United States collaborated in order to make their warning to Japan more effective, and on December 5, 1935, simultaneous declarations were made in London and Washington, pointing out in effect that China's territorial and administrative integrity and the Open Door were in danger of being impaired by Japanese activities. These protests and warnings were, however, entirely ineffective, because the Japanese Government invariably took the positions that it had nothing to do with the events. Whatever the acutal Japanese replies, of more importance was the basic Japanese attitude of refusal to take up the question of treaty rights and obligations in view of the changes in the actual situation—changes which the protesting powers refused to recognize.

What made relations between Japan and the two Anglo-Saxon countries still worse was the Japanese notification to the United States Government on December 29, 1934 of its intention to terminate the Washington Naval Treaty and the failure of the London Naval Conference of 1935 to reach any new agreement. This conference opened on December 6, 1935 and practically ended on January 15, 1936 when the Japanese delegation formally withdrew. Thus the year 1937 began without any naval limitation treaties whatever in the Pacific area. The stumbling block of the London conference was the conflict of opinion over the ratio principle : Japan persistently demanded its replacement by a "common upper limit" of global tonnage for all powers, whereas Great Britain and the United States with equal persistence insisted upon its continuation. The circumstances in which Japan dared to withdraw from the conference were perhaps most frankly explained by the following words of Admiral Nagano, Chief Delegate of Japan ; "The situation of Japan and the Far East is such as would absolutely forbid the continuation of the ratio principle of the Washington and London naval limitation treaties. Because of these treaties, various regrettable questions have recurred in Japan and in the Far East. Japan is now firmly determined not to give up her fundamental claim for a 'common upper limit'."

The outlook for international relations in the Pacific was thus gradually becoming darker, but until the outbreak of Sino-Japanese hostilities Japan's relations with both Great Britain and the United States remained comparatively tranquil. Great Britain especially was not only inclined to seek some sort of understanding with Japan in view of the threatening offensive of Germany and Italy in Europe, but was even impressed by the report, submitted by Sir Frederick Leith-Ross on his return home, which contained recommendations for Anglo-Japanese cooperation in China. Informal feelers were actually put out by diplomats in London, although the existing situation did not permit of any fruitful diplomatic negotiations. The United States on the other hand continued to adhere to a negative attitude towards the Far East as well as Europe, since isolationist sentiments remained dominant within the country.

Even the outbreak of the Lukouchiao Incident did not immediately precipitate matters. On July 16, Secretary of State Hull issued a statement, indicating the American attitude towards the imminent menace of war. He avoided referring to any treaty or any country by name, and in extremely cautious words, he defined the general principles of the American peace policy such as " faithful observance of international agreements ", " adjustment of problems in international relations by processes of peaceful negotiation and agreement ", or " cooperative effort by peaceful and practicable means " and tried to rouse public opinion in the world. To this declaration of American policy, Japan responded by pointing out that in the application of the general principles of the Hull statement to the Far Eastern situation, " a full recognition and practical consideration of the actual particular circumstances of that region " was necessary.

Great Britain was particularly distressed by the sudden change in the North China situation, inasmuch as she had been anxious to help China achieve internal unity while seeking rapprochement with Japan. She was even reported to have advised the Nanking Government to accept the local settlement of the Lukouchiao Incident.

In the latter half of 1937, strong public pressure in the United States was brought upon the Government for the enforcement of the Neutrality Act, but the Government elected to let its policy " remain on a 24-hour basis ". On September 14, it was announced that American vessels should not transport to China or Japan any armaments " which were listed in the

President's proclamation of May 1, 1937", and that "any other merchant vessels, flying the American flag, which attempt[ed] to transport any of the listed articles to China or Japan [would] do so at their own risk",—a policy which in effect was more disadvantageous to China. On September 22, on the occasion of Japanese air raids on Nanking, the American Government protested to Japan against any bombing of "an extensive area wherein there resides a large populace engaged in peaceful pursuits" and declared that it would reserve all rights in respect of damages which might result. Foreign Minister Hirota explained on September 29 that the bombing was necessitated for military purposes; non-combatants would not be attacked; the rights and interests of third countries would be respected as far as possible; and yet damages might be unavoidable.

China appealed to the League of Nations. Her first statement was presented on August 20, 1937, and another supplementary one on September 12. In the latter, after describing the development of the fighting, the Chinese Government declared : "It is further demonstrated by the above-mentioned facts that the Japanese armed forces, in invading China's territory, show utter disregard for all rules of international law and provisions of treaties and all precepts of humanity." On September 15, the Japanese Government released a counter-statement by the Foreign Office spokesman, in which it made clear its attitude towards the Chinese appeal by saying : "As Japan, not being a member of the League of Nations, has maintained a policy of non-cooperation with the League on political matters, she is not in a position to have any concern with arguments made in the League meetings, even though China has made an appeal to the League." The statement then proceeded to point out various Chinese distortions of facts and declared that the policy of the Japanese Government in dealing with the present China Affair was to make China abandon her mistaken policy of anti-Japanism and thus to bring about " a fundamental adjustment of Sino-Japanese relations ".

The Council of the League of Nations referred the case to its Far Eastern Advisory Committee of twenty-three countries on September 16, and accepted the two reports of the Committee on October 6. One of the reports recommended that a Nine-Power conference should be convened. The Assembly also adopted the following resolution in accordance with the recommendation : " The Assembly. . . expresses its moral support for China and recommends that members of the League should. . . consider how far they can individually extend aid to China." On the previous day (October 5), the President of the United States had delivered an address in Chicago, expounding the much talked-of " quarantine " policy —an address which may be regarded as an indication of American cooperation with the League of Nations. A few days later, on October 12, in a much milder " fireside chat ", the President stated that the American Government had accepted an invitation to the Brussels Conference because it concurred with the aim of the Conference to seek a solution of the conflict " by agreement " and because it wanted to cooperate in this work with other signatory powers of the Nine-Power Treaty. The most important aspect of the " chat " was the indication that the American Government was not contemplating anything more drastic than mediation. This ruled out, therefore, the possibility of American participation in some sort of coercive action, which seemed implied in the Chicago speech.

The severest blow to the Brussels Conference was Japan's refusal to participate. The Japanese Government " adhered firmly to the view that their present action, being one of self-defence forced upon Japan by the challenge of China [lay] outside the scope of the Nine-Power Treaty.... ". " It [was] certainly impossible for them to accept an invitation to a conference convened in accordance with the stipulations of that treaty after Japan [had] been accused of having violated its terms." In such circumstances the best the Conference could hope to achieve was to mobilize public opinion in the world and to establish anew the principles of regulating the actions of nations. That it would not directly affect the Sino-Japanese conflict had been expected. After the Conference, however, British policy seems to have undergone some modification, being freed from any obligations imposed by the League of Nations Covenant. She appeared thereafter to reconsider her policy of assisting China from her own standpoint, especially that of protecting her rights and interests in that country. Consequently, she came to adopt a more truly neutral policy towards the two belligerents.

As the area of fighting was extended, the damage which the Sino-Japanese conflict inflicted on foreign interests in China also became greater and more serious. The most serious cases were perhaps those of the *Ladybird* and the *Panay* on December 5 and 12, 1937, respectively. Supported by an aroused public opinion, both the American and the British Governments formally approached the Japanese Government in an especially strong manner, the procedure of the former being reported to have been quite unusual. The Japanese Government and people greatly regretted the occurrence of such incidents, and the Government formally expressed sincere apologies and promised indemnification for losses and punishment of those responsible. As indicated by the settlement of the *Panay* Incident, the American Government avoided any positive intervention and instead, while watching the development of the conflict with great concern, kept lodging protests with the Japanese Government whenever American rights and interests were endangered. The note of May 31, 1938, regarding the status of American property in China occupied by the Japanese forces, may be regarded as the most representative of the numerous, minor protests.

However, the American note of October 6, 1938, regarding Japanese violation of American rights in China was not only the longest, but the most important one, involving the fundamental questions of the Open Door principle and the status of the rights and interests of third powers in the occupied area of China. The Japanese reply was delayed until after the Government had decided upon the basic policy of the settlement of the China Affair on November 3. On November 18, after Foreign Minister Arita secured its approval by the Cabinet and the Emperor, it was handed to Eugene Dooman, American *Chargé d'affaires* in Tokyo. This reply was a highly significant document in that it proclaimed to the world the new Japanese policy concerning the establishment of a new order in East Asia, and frankly stated that " in the face of the new situation. . . any attempt to apply to the conditions of to-day and to-morrow inapplicable ideas and principles of the past [would not] solve the immediate issues ". We shall refer to it more fully in Chapter XIII.

The British Government also presented protests to the Japanese Government, including one regarding the closing of the Yangtze under the date of November 7. In the meantime the British Government was seeking conferences with the Japanese Government with a view to settling specific outstanding questions without touching upon the major and fundamental issue of policy. But, as in the case of the American presentations, the Japanese Government had not been in a position to give any definite response before it decided upon the new policy on November 3.

CHAPTER XII

STATEMENTS OF THE JAPANESE GOVERN-
MENT REGARDING THE NEW ORDER
IN EAST ASIA

The Ultimate Japanese Objective in the China Affair

For more than a year after the outbreak of the China Affair, the Japanese Government did not proclaim its ultimate war aims, save that it intended to " chastise " the anti-Japanese policy of China by means of armed forces. Perhaps the Government had no time to contemplate anything more serious or fundamental. In any case, as is clear from the circumstances in which the fighting broke out, the antagonism between the two countries had reached such a point that Japan was simply driven to defend herself against the overwhelming force of an anti-Japanese China. And once fighting had started, Japan could not stop half way, no matter how fervently she wished to prevent it from being aggravated or to avoid the undesirable " by-products " of an extensive war.

At the same time it was clear that the basic cause of the clash lay in the conflict of policy in the past, especially over the status of North China. And it was presently also made clear that the outbreak of war had neither changed Japan's policy as regards North China nor the principles of her China policy as indicated in the Hirota formula. This was evident in the peace terms which the Japanese Government formulated when the German Government offered to mediate—terms which Foreign Minister Hirota disclosed on January 20, 1938.

During the first year of hostilities, therefore, the Japanese plan for settlement was the same as that for the settlement of the North China problem.   Essentially it was a continuation of her policy for the settlement of the Manchurian problem. In other words, it consisted in the establishment of a new order in North China and Inner Mongolia, contiguous to Manchoukuo, which would be somewhat similar to, if not identical with, that of the new state.

It will be recalled that the successive Governments in Japan had attempted in vain to combine this North China policy with one of conciliation and of cooperation with the rest of China.   Prime Minister Prince Konoye, especially after the outbreak of war, while determined to fight through till the end, seems to have contemplated something more drastic, yet more rational, than either the Hirota principles or the North China formula—something by which a fundamental readjustment of Sino-Japanese relations might be brought about.   It was a gigantic task, but throughout the spring of 1938, the idea was being gradually formulated in his mind, and preparations were steadily in progress.

The first indication was the unprecedentedly far-reaching reorganization of the Cabinet, carried out soon after the fall of Hsuchow on May 25, 1938.   The extent to which the Cabinet was strengthened, and to which this added to the confidence of the nation, was quite considerable. The next indication was the commencement of preparations by the War, Navy and Foreign Offices for a central institution to be entrusted with the task of rehabilitating the occupied areas— preparations which bore fruit when the China Affairs Board was inaugurated on December 16, 1938.   All this time voices were growing more clamorous, insisting that the Government define its war aims in the light of new developments of the war, and decide whether Japan was to carry on the prolonged war which she had neither planned nor desired.   The time now appeared ripe for the Government to launch a new policy for the settlement of the China Affair.

Thus, fittingly enough, on November 3, 1938, a day set aside in commemoration of the Emperor Meiji, the whole nation, which was still celebrating the great victories at Canton (October 22) and Hankow (October 25), was informed through the press and the radio that the ultimate aim of the present campaign was the establishment of " a New Order in East Asia ". The full text of the statement issued by the Japanese Government on that day follows :

" By the august virtue of His Majesty, our naval and military forces have captured Canton and the three cities of Wuhan ; and all the vital areas of China have thus fallen into our hands. The Kuomintang Government exists no longer except as a mere local regime. However, so long as it persists in its anti-Japanese and pro-communist policy our country will not lay down its arms— never until that regime is crushed.

What Japan seeks is the establishment of a new order which will insure the permanent stability of East Asia. In this lies the ultimate purpose of our present military campaign.

This new order has for its foundation a tripartite relationship of mutual aid and co-ordination between Japan, Manchoukuo and China in political, economic, cultural and other fields. Its object is to secure international justice, to perfect the joint defence against Communism, and to create a new culture and realize a close economic cohesion throughout East Asia. This indeed is the way to contribute towards the stabilization of East Asia and the progress of the world.

What Japan desires of China is that that country will share in the task of bringing about this new order in East Asia. She confidently expects that the people of China will fully comprehend her true intentions and that they will respond to the call of Japan for their cooperation. Even the participation of the Kuomintang Government would not be rejected, if, repudiating the policy which has guided it in the past and remoulding its personnel, so as to translate its rebirth into fact, it were to come forward to join in the establishment of the new order.

Japan is confident that other Powers will on their part correctly appreciate her aims and policy and adapt their attitude to the new conditions prevailing in East Asia. For the cordiality hitherto manifested by the nations which are in sympathy with us, Japan wishes to express her profound gratitude.

The establishment of a new order in East Asia is in complete conformity with the very spirit in which the Empire was founded; to achieve such a task is the exalted responsibility with which our present generation is entrusted. It is, therefore, imperative to carry out all necessary internal reforms, and with a full development of the aggregate national strength, material as well as moral, fulfil at all costs this duty incumbent upon our nation.

This, the Government declares to be the immutable policy and determination of Japan. "

This is a proclamation of the idealistic settlement of the China Affair, the aspiration of the people and the Government of Japan. Its essence lies in the proposition that a lasting peace between Japan and China shall transcend all the old grievances and the new, and all of the actual situations which have been created or are being created by the war. It is an attempt seriously to re-examine all developments since the Manchurian Incident which have directly or indirectly led to the break down of Sino-Japanese relations, and yet to search for a new world in which the two peoples can live together. Reading between the lines, one may discern the realization that one cause of the conflict lies in a collision of two different policies, that another lies in the semi-colonization of China brought about by the impact of the West on the East, that still another lies in the dependence of Japan herself upon the Western powers. But, most important of all, one may discern the realization that the greatest cause of the conflict lies in deep-rooted distrust and uncompromising self-confidence of the two peoples so that neither of them has ever thought of joining hands with the other to find a common ground for existence and prosperity.   Such is the background of the conception of " a New Order in East Asia ".   Partly a product of the intelligence and imagination of the people, partly a product of the high calibre and character of the Konoye Cabinet and especially of its leader, this conception is now embodied in an epoch-making official statement, the realization of which is the ultimate aim of the China Affair.

Closely related to this idea of a new order is the idea of " international justice " referred to in the same statement ; for the realization of international justice is one of the foremost objectives of the new order in East Asia.   That the establishment of international justice is urgently desired by Japan was emphatically stated by Prime Minister Prince Konoye in a radio address delivered on the day as the statement was issued.

" What the world needs today is a lasting peace based upon a foundation of justice and fair dealing.   It cannot be denied that the principles governing international relations in the recent past have in practice tended only to preserve and perpetuate with cast-iron rigidity an inequitable state of affairs.   In this irrational arrangement lies the fundamental cause of the collapse of the Covenant of the League of Nations along with many other pacts and treaties.   We should not allow international justice to remain merely a beautiful phrase, but we should strive to create a new framework of peace, in accordance with a comprehensive view of all human activities such as commerce, emigration, natural resources and culture ; and in keeping with the actual conditions and the progress of events I firmly believe that this is the only way to overcome the universal crisis which confronts us today. "

It is true that the Government statement of November 3 includes specific proposals which reminds one of Hirota's three principles and accordingly it is not a result of entirely original deliberations.   But its true importance does not lie so much in these specific proposals as in the expression of Japan's desire that China " will share in the task of bringing about a new order in East Asia ", or in the earnest suggestion that the Kuomintang Government " come forward to join in the establishment of the new order ", " repudiating the policy which has guided it in the past and remoulding its personnel ". It is not a mere diplomatic paper, but rather a declaration, beyond the sphere of diplomacy, of a common objective to be striven for jointly by the two peoples. And therein lies the historic significance of the statement as well as the uncommon nature of the war settlement contemplated by Japan. If a mere statement of the Konoye Cabinet cannot possibly attain this objective with one stroke, it is at least an effort to that end and, in that sense, historians of the future will not fail to re-estimate its value.

Reactions within the country to this statement were of two kinds. While some people doubted, in view of the superiority complex of the Japanese, the practicability of such an idealistic or rational design of Sino-Japanese cooperation for " commonweal ", others were encouraged precisely by its idealistic or rational nature hoping that it might succeed in breaking through the hopeless impasse which every other means had failed to surmount. This difference of opinion will undoubtedly be precipitated when the time comes to draw up concrete peace terms in accordance with this plan.

Proposed Terms of Readjustment of Sino-Japanese Relations

The main purpose of the November 3 statement of the Japanese Government was to respond to the national demand for a guiding principle for settlement of the China Affair. It was, therefore, essentially addressed to the Japanese public. In order to appeal directly to the Chinese people, Japanese " peace terms " should be made known. In order to convince the world at large, especially those third countries having interests in China, more specific elucidation of the new order should be made public. The Japanese Government partially did this, when it published Premier Konoye's statement of December 22, 1938. This was a proclamation of the Japanese Government's basic policy for readjustment of Sino-Japanese relations. It is what has since been known as the " Konoye Statement " ; it is also what Wang Ching-wei, since he inaugurated his peace movement, has always referred to as Japanese " peace terms ". It reads as follows :

" The Japanese Government are resolved, as has been clearly set forth in their two previous statements issued this year, to carry on the military operations for the complete extermination of the anti-Japanese Kuomintang Government, and at the same time to proceed with the work of establishing a new order in East Asia together with those far-sighted Chinese who share in our ideals and aspirations.

The spirit of renaissance is now sweeping over all parts of China and enthusiasm for reconstruction is mounting ever higher. The Japanese Government desire to make public their basic policy for adjusting the relations between Japan and China, in order that their intentions may be thoroughly understood both at home and abroad.

Japan, China and Manchoukuo will be united by the common aim of establishing the new order in East Asia and of realizing a relationship of neighbourly amity, common defence against Communism, and economic cooperation. For that purpose it is necessary first of all that China should cast aside all narrow and prejudiced views belonging to the past and do away with the folly of anti-Japanism, and resentment regarding Manchoukuo. In other words, Japan frankly desires China to enter of her own will into complete diplomatic relations with Manchoukuo.

The existence of the Comintern influence in East Asia cannot be tolerated. The Japanese therefore consider it an essential condition of the adjustment of Sino-Japanese relations that there should be concluded an anti-Comintern agreement between the two countries in consonance with the spirit of the Anti-Comintern Agreement between Japan, Germany and Italy. And in order to ensure the full accomplishment of her purpose, Japan demands, in view of the actual circumstances prevailing in China, that Japanese troops be stationed, as an anti-Communist measure, at specified points during the time the said agreement is in force, and also that the Inner Mongolian region be designated as a special anti-Communist area.

As regards economic relations between the two countries, Japan does not intend to exercise economic monopoly in China, nor does she intend to demand of China to limit the interests of those third Powers who grasp the meaning of the new East Asia and are willing to act accordingly. Japan only seeks to render effective the co-operation and collaboration between the two countries. That is to say, Japan demands that China, in accordance with the principle of equality between the two countries, should recognize the freedom of residence and trade on the part of Japanese subjects in the interior of China, with a view to promoting the economic interests of both peoples; and that, in the light of the historical and economic relations between the two nations, China should extend to Japan facilities for the development of China's natural resources, especially in the regions of North China and Inner Mongolia.

The above gives the general lines of what Japan demands of China. If the true object of Japan in conducting the present vast military campaign be fully understood, it will be plain that what she seeks is neither territory nor indemnity for the costs of military operations. Japan demands only the minimum guarantee needed for the execution by China of her function as a participant in the establishment of the new order.

Japan not only respects the sovereignty of China, but she is prepared to give positive consideration to the questions of the abolition of extra-territoriality and of the rendition of concessions and settlements—matters which are necessary for the full independence of China. "

A close examination of this document will show that an

adjustment is sought between the demands which Japan has hitherto urged on China and the counter-claims which China has invariably put forward. Japan is now presenting only those demands which she cannot forego and is assuring China that these are the minimum conditions necessary for the establishment of the proposed new relationship between the two countries. At the same time Japan offers to have the fullest and highest respect for the Chinese demand for independence and territorial and administrative integrity.

Specifically, Japan's minimum demands are (1) establishment of friendly relations between China and Manchoukuo; (2) conclusion of a Sino-Japanese anti-Comintern agreement, stationing of Japanese troops at specified points, and designation of Inner Mongolia as a special anti-Communist area; (3) the grant of facilities to Japan in the development of natural resources in North China and Inner Mongolia. This is what is implied in the three principles of the new order: (1) neighbourly friendship; (2) joint defence against communism; and (3) economic cooperation.

This statement has been received by the Japanese public more or less in the same way as the previous one was. In particular the principle of " no annexations, no indemnities ", which is explicitly stated there, has been regarded with rather strong disfavour by those who advocate conquest of China in the fullest sense of the term or those who believe that the cost of war can be repaid in the material sense. This school of thought was reflected in some of the discussions held in the 74th Diet in January–March 1939, but the Government at that time, as invariably since then, upheld the principle proclaimed in the statement.

The terms of the statement are, naturally, still very general, and when it is further elaborated and specified, as undoubtedly it will be, it may be modified or altered to a greater or less extent according to the existing circumstances. But it is expected that any such modifications or alterations, whatever direction they may take, will not substantially affect the fundamental principles underlying the statement, because these principles are regarded as the minimum requisite for true cooperation between Japan and China, after taking into serious consideration the limits and nature of the Chinese demands on the one hand and the possibility of controlling various popular demands prevailing in Japan on the other.

After the resignation of the Konoye Cabinet, by which these basic principles were formulated, the Government rapidly changed hands from Baron Hiranuma to General Abe, from General Abe to Admiral Yonai, and it does not seem that the Yonai Cabinet will last long. But it seems sufficiently safe to expect that, in spite of these Cabinet changes, this "immutable national policy" will truly remain immutable, or, more correctly, it is scarcely expected that, as far as Japan is concerned, there should be any such change in the political situation as would undermine these basic principles. The question seems to be, not the possibility of any change in these principles, but rather the circumstances in which, and the procedure under which, they will be realized. And this will depend above anything else upon the actual circumstances which will prevail in China and among third powers.

CHAPTER XIII

THE NEW ORDER IN EAST ASIA AND THIRD POWERS

Japanese Policy as Indicated in the Reply to the U.S.A.

While the Japanese Government was deliberating upon the basic principles of the Far Eastern new order, actual conditions in China were rapidly changing. Over one year had elapsed since the outbreak of the war; two Chinese regimes and various other minor organizations had been set up in the areas occupied by the Japanese troops; economic and strategic measures of various kinds had been taken, necessarily affecting the positions of third powers in China, based upon treaties or otherwise. And reference has been made already in preceding chapters to the notices or protests presented by the British and the American Governments regarding such conditions.

One of the impending tasks of the Japanese Government was to deal with these specific questions, and in such a way as would not seriously contradict the fundamental policy which it had now adopted for the construction of a new order in East Asia. And yet the Foreign Office, whose job it was to do so, was not in a position to estimate or ascertain the degree and possibility of permanency of various actions and situations which have been temporarily brought about for military purposes. One may well imagine how difficult it was in such circumstances to undertake diplomatic negotiations at all, and, still more, to achieve success in such negotiations.

This at least partially explains the delay of the Japanese Government's reply to the American note of October 6, 1938. In its final reply, however, the Japanese Government for the first time expressed its official view of the specific questions raised by the American Government, such as that of export exchange measures at Tsingtao, tariff revisions, American rights and interests, return of American citizens to occupied areas, treatment of Americans, etc., and also of the relation between the new order and the nationals of third powers. The full text of the Japanese reply was as follows :

" Excellency,

I have the honour to acknowledge the receipt of Your Excellency's Note, No. 1076, dated October 6th, addressed to the then Minister for Foreign Affairs Prince Konoye, concerning the rights and interests of the United States in China.

In the Note are cited various instances based on information in the possession of the Government of the United States that the Japanese authorities are subjecting American citizens in China to discriminatory treatment and violating the rights and interests of the United States.

I have now the honour to state hereunder the opinions of the Japanese Government with regard to these instances.

1) The circumstances which led to the adoption of the present measures concerning export exchange in Tsingtao and the present situation being, so far as the Japanese Government are aware, as set forth below, they consider that those measures can not be construed as constituting any discrimination against American citizens.

A short time ago the Federal Reserve Bank of China was established in North China whose notes with an exchange value fixed at one shilling and two pence against one yuan, have been issued thus far to the amount of more than one hundred million yuan, and are widely circulated. These bank notes being the compulsory currency of the Provisional Government, the maintenance of their value and their smooth circulation is regarded as an indispensable basis for the conduct and the development of economic activities in North China. Consequently the Japanese Government have taken a cooperative attitude ; and all Japanese subjects are using the said notes, and in their export trade are exchanging them at the rate of one shilling and two pence. On the other hand, the old *fa-pi* still circulating in these areas has depreciated in exchange value to about eight pence per yuan. Consequently those who are engaged in export trade and are using this currency are enjoying illegitimate profits, as compared with those who use the Federal Reserve notes and carry on legitimate transactions at the legitimate rate of exchange : that is to say, Japanese subjects who use the Federal Reserve notes have been suffering unreasonable disadvantages as compared with persons who, while residing and carrying on their business in the areas under the jurisdiction of the Provisional Government of North China, use, nevertheless, the old *fa-pi* exclusively.

Furthermore, the existence of the before-mentioned disparity in exchange value between the new notes and the old *fa-pi*, which the Federal Reserve Bank has been exchanging at a rate not very much below par, is bound to exert an unfavourable effect upon the exchange value of the new notes, and eventually upon the exchange value of the Japanese yen.

The Japanese Government feel that it is incumbent upon them not to remain indifferent to such a situation.

The export exchange measures adopted in Tsingtao are calculated to place the users of old Chinese currency who have been obtaining unfair profits, on equal footing with those who are using the Federal Reserve notes. These measures are also intended to protect the exchange value of the Federal Reserve Bank notes. Inasmuch as the application of the measures makes no differentiation according to nationality they cannot be considered as discriminatory measures. As a matter of fact, it is through these measures that those users of the Federal Reserve notes who had in a sense been discriminated against, have been placed on an equal footing with the others, and thus enabled to compete on a fair basis.

2) In North and Central China the new Chinese regimes some time ago effected revisions of the Customs tariff in an attempt to secure a rational modification of the former tariff enforced by the Kuomintang Government, which was unduly high and ill-calculated

to promote the economic recovery and general welfare of the Chinese people. However, the schedule actually adopted for the time being is the one that was approved by the Powers in 1931, so that no complaint has been heard from foreign residents of any nationality on the spot. The Japanese Government are of course in favour of the purpose of the said revision, believing that it will serve to promote effectively the trade of all countries with China.

3) As for the organization of certain promotion companies in China, the restoration and development of China's economic, financial and industrial life after the present Affair is a matter of urgent necessity for the welfare of the Chinese. Moreover, the Japanese Government are deeply solicitous for the early inauguration and progress of work having for its object this restoration and development, for the sake of the realization of a new order in East Asia, and are doing all in their power in that direction. The North China Development Company and the Central China Development Company were established with a view to giving China the necessary assistance towards the said restoration and also with the aim of contributing towards the development of China's natural resources. It is far from the thought of the Japanese Government to impair the rights and interests of American citizens in China or to discriminate against their enterprises. The Japanese Government therefore do not oppose, but welcome heartily, the participation of third Powers on the basis of the new situation that has arisen.

The telecommunication companies in North and Central China, the Inland Navigation Steamship Company at Shanghai and the wharfage company at Tsingtao have also been established to meet the imperative need of an early restoration of communications, transportation, and harbour facilities. With the exception of the telecommunications enterprise, which, because of its obvious relation to the maintenance of peace and order and to the national defence, as well as because of its public character, has been placed in the hands of special companies, all these enterprises are turned over to concerns that are ordinary Chinese or Japanese juridical persons, without any intention of allowing them to reap monopolistic profits by discriminating against the United States or any other Power.   As regards the wool trade, while the control of purchasing agencies was enforced for a time in the Mongolian region, it has since been discontinued.   There is no plan at present of any sort for establishing a monopoly in tobacco.

4)   Concerning the return of American citizens to the occupied areas, Your Excellency is aware that in North China there is no restriction, excepting in very special cases where the personal safety of those who return would be endangered, while in the Yangtze Valley large numbers of Americans have already returned. The reason why permission to return has not yet been made general is, as has been repeatedly communicated to Your Excellency, due to the danger that persists because of the imperfect restoration of order and also to the impossibility of admitting nationals of third Powers on account of strategic necessities such as the preservation of military secrets.   Again, the various restrictions enforced in the occupied areas concerning the residence, travel, enterprise and trade of American citizens, constitute the minimum regulations possible consistently with military necessities and the local conditions of peace and order.   It is the intention of the Japanese Government to restore the situation to normal as soon as circumstances permit.

5)   The Japanese Government are surprised at the allegation that there exist a fundamental difference between the treatment accorded to Japanese in America and the treatment accorded to Americans in Japan.   While it is true that in these days of emergency Americans residing in this country are subject to various economic restrictions, yet these are, needless to say, restrictions imposed not upon Americans alone but also on all foreigners of all nationalities as well as upon the subjects of Japan.   I beg to reserve for another occasion a statement of the views of the Japanese Government concerning the treatment of Japanese subjects in American territory, referred to in Your Excellency's note.

As has been explained above, the Japanese Government, with every intention of fully respecting American rights and interests in China, have been doing all that could possibly be done in that behalf.   However, since there are in progress at present in China military operations on a scale unprecedented in our history, it may well be recognized by the Government of the United States that it is unavoidable that these military operations should occasionally present obstacles to giving full effect to our intention of respecting the rights and interests of American citizens.

Japan at present is devoting her energy to the establishment of a new order based on genuine international justice throughout East Asia, the attainment of which end is not only an indispensable condition of the very existence of Japan, but also constitutes the very foundation of the enduring peace and stability of East Asia.

It is the firm conviction of the Japanese Government that in the face of the new situation, fast developing in East Asia, any attempt to apply to the conditions of to-day and to-morrow inapplicable ideas and principles of the past would neither contribute towards the establishment of a real peace in East Asia nor solve the immediate issues.

However, as long as these points are understood, Japan has not the slightest inclination to oppose the participation of the United States and other Powers in the great work of reconstructing East Asia along all lines of industry and trade ; and I believe that the new regimes now being formed in China are prepared to welcome such foreign participation.

I avail myself of this opportunity to renew to Your Excellency the assurances of my highest consideration. "

To the allegations concerning discriminations against American nationals, special rights given exclusively to Japanese, monopolies contrary to the principle of equal opportunity, etc., the Japanese Government replied in essence, first, that Americans alone were not being discriminated against, but all other third powers were treated in the same way and, second, that some of the special rights and monopolies should be recognized as the results of the special relations between Japan and China resulting from the new situation in the Far East—a theory incompatible with the principles of the

Nine-Power Treaty. The concluding part of the reply indicated this Japanese attitude.

Foreign Policy toward a New Order in East Asia

Japan did not declare war on China, nor has the declaration of a new order been accepted by third powers. Consequently the new situation now in existence in China does not alter the existing order *per se*. It may be only natural, therefore, that the United States and other countries should still not be satisfied by the Japanese view as indicated in the Japanese reply to the United States note. In particular, the Japanese claim for exceptions to the principles of the Open Door and equal opportunity, though understandable from Japan's standpoint, is not acceptable to third powers.

With a view to obtaining an understanding by the British and the American Governments of the intended new order, Foreign Minister Arita commenced free conversations with the Ambassadors of both countries on December 8, 1938. He explained the real intentions of the Japanese Government regarding the principles of the Open Door and equal opportunity in China, emphasizing the fact that in the future, in accordance with the principle of free competition and equal opportunity, the economic activities of third powers in China would receive non-discriminatory treatment with Japan, so long as this did not imperil in any way the independence and autonomy of China. The main points in Japan's conception of the new order as elucidated by the Foreign Minister were as follows :

1) Japan fervently desires to bring about the stability of East Asia which has been a common aspiration of Japan, Manchoukuo and China.

2) One condition necessary for that stability is that these three countries should be enabled adequately to defend themselves against the Communist menace. China, however, is actually under the influence of Communism at least partially and is not likely

to be strong enough to overcome it. Since such a situation immediately threatens the peace and security of Japan and Manchoukuo, Japan is impelled, either from that standpoint or from
that of rescuing China herself, to urge China to cooperate with
her against the spread of the red menace.

3) In view of the world-wide tendency towards economic
autarchy, economic cooperation between Japan and China is not
only necessary and imperative, but advantageous to China because it would ensure a market for her natural products and
materials. The National Government, however, has refused to
see this mutually complementary relationship of both countries
and has tended to disregard the vital interest of Japan. Therein
must be found at least one cause of the present conflict. This
country is determined to remove whatever obstacles exist to this
Sino-Japanese economic cooperation.

4) By regaining tariff autonomy, China has improved her financial and economic condition, and attained some of the conditions
of an independent state, but is still at a serious disadvantage because of the unequal treaties, the Nine-Power Treaty and various
loan contracts of a markedly political nature. Consequently, China
will be obliged, for the immediate future, to be retarded in her recovery from war damages, and will, as long as such handi-
caps exist, continue to be a semi-colonial market for the Western
powers. Clearly, the existence of such a China will not be conducive to the stability of East Asia. It must certainly be considered abnormal that any independent state should be sacrificed
to the interest of other countries and consequently not allowed
freely to carry out necessary policies, internally or externally, to
promote its vital interest and economic security. The powers
have agreed in principle to the abolition of extra-territoriality in
accordance with China's desire, but this has not been realized yet.
Either for the interest of China herself or for the stability of East
Asia, Japan will comply at the earliest opportunity with the Chinese
desire in this connection. Other countries, too, are advised to
cooperate in discontinuing the present situation where China's
independence is restricted by extraterritoriality, the unequal
treaties, the Nine-Power Treaty and various contracts.

5) It is clear that the foreign interests which would exist in China after the removal of the present abnormal condition should be more or less the same as those now existing in Japan, Great Britain, the United States, etc. Inasmuch as Japan stands in such a relationship to China that one country vitally affects the other economically and strategically, the extent of cooperation between them in the fields of national defence, politics and economics should naturally be greater than that of cooperation between China and other countries. And, as a matter of fact, a similar state of affairs does exist, to a greater or less extent, in other parts of the world. Needless to say, Japan does not intend to exclude the economic activities of the Western peoples or deprive them of their trading freedom in China.

6) Only when, the above-mentioned conditions have been realized and China thus has fully recovered her independence, and not till then, will the Far Eastern stability which Japan is striving for be attained. The Nine-Power Treaty was originally concluded on the condition that it would in no way hinder China from promoting her vital interest and economic security. Therefore, to the degree to which China grows as an independent state and needs to widen the field in which to exercise administrative powers, the principle of equal opportunity of the Treaty will be found an obstacle; accordingly the scope of its application should be narrowed. Every country would admit this, even if there were no special relationship between Japan and China. And that a special relationship between Japan and China should be recognized is a necessity vital to both countries, and if other countries do not recognize this, it is tantamount to denying Japan and China the right to live.

7) The principle of equal opportunity upheld in the Nine-Power Treaty may be interpreted as one which prevents the growth of such relationship and thus secures China as a semi-colonial market for the Western powers. If so, it would not only interfere with Japan's right to live, but obstruct China's administrative powers in the economic field. It would thus impede the growth as a state of both Japan and China. It would certainly not be applicable to the new situation in East Asia.

8) In consequence, the future activities of other countries in trade, enterprises and capital investments in China should not be conducted in accordance with the provisions of the Nine-Power Treaty, but should be restricted within such bounds that the special relations between Japan and China are recognized and China's independence unimpeded. Specifically : (a) the economic activities of other countries in China should not conflict with China's basic requirements of national defence. This is a matter of great concern for Japan, since China is to be an important participant with Japan and Manchoukuo in the joint defence of East Asia against the Communist menace. Thus no treaty should in any way hinder (i) development of natural resources and certain raw materials (cotton, wool, salt, etc.) ; (ii) control of railways, harbours, shipping, roads, air-routes, communications ; (iii) management of the munition industries and power industries (electricity industry, etc.). (b) The economic activities of other countries in China should not impede China's administrative powers in the economic sphere. (c) Except for the above two items, other countries will be treated with equality and without discrimination.

9) In short, the economic activities of other countries in China in the future should be subjected to the " restrictions dictated by the requirements of the national defence and economic security of the countries grouped under the new order, and no political privileges should be attached to those activities ". Otherwise other countries will enjoy in the Chinese market freedom of trade, enterprise and investment as well as non-discriminatory treatment. In other words, other countries in China will be entitled to the same freedom which any given independent state in the West is granting to foreigners with due restrictions dictated by its own needs.

10) As often stated since the outbreak of the present conflict, the Japanese Government will respect the economic activities of other countries in China and their rights and interests based upon those activities. However, this does not mean that it will respect all the existing foreign interests, but that it will be held responsible for the losses incurred to those foreign interests which will be existing after due adjustments have been made in the light of the

new situation in East Asia.

With reference to these conversations and the Japanese reply of November 18, the American and the British Governments presented their rebuttals on December 31, 1938 and January 14, 1939, respectively. The tone of these notes was extremely forceful, as if challenging the firm determination of Japan to carry out her declared policy.

The first point in the second American note was that the " imposition of restrictions upon the movements and activities of American nationals ... has placed, and will, if continued increasingly, place Japanese interests in a preferred position, and is therefore unquestionably discriminatory in its effect against legitimate American interests ". Further, such matters as exchange control, compulsory currency circulation, tariff remission, etc. ... "imply an assumption ... that the regimes established and maintained in China by Japanese armed forces are entitled to act in China in a capacity such as flows from rights of sovereignty " and would in effect be " disregarding " the rights and interests of other countries. Therefore the American Government " expresses its conviction that [such] restrictions ... are not only unjust and unwarranted, but counter to ... the international agreements ".

The second point was that the Japanese Government appeared to " affirm that it is its intention to make its [oft-reiterated] observance of treaty obligations conditional upon an understanding by the American Government and by other Governments of a new situation and a new order in the Far East as envisaged and fostered by Japanese authorities. " but that such " admonition " is " highly paradoxical ".

Thirdly, America's " adherence to and its advocacy of the principle of equality of opportunity do not flow solely from a desire to obtain the commercial benefits ", but also from a

" firm conviction " that they lead to internal and international stability. " The people and the Government of the United States could not agree to the establishment at the instance of and for the special purposes of any Third Country of a new regime which would arbitrarily deprive them of the long established rights of equal opportunity and fair treatment which are legally and justly theirs . . . . "

Fourthly, according to the view of the Japanese Government, the " conditions of today and tomorrow call for a revision of the ideas and principles of the past ", but the American Government had expressed its opinion on April 29, 1934, with reference to the Amau statement that " Treaties can lawfully be modified or be terminated . . . only by processes prescribed or recognized or agreed upon by the parties to them ". During recent decades Japan and the United States have often conferred and have invariably come to an agreement in these matters. " This Government is well aware that the situation has changed. " " This Government does not admit, however, that there is need or warrant for any one Power to take upon itself to prescribe what shall be the terms and conditions of a new order in areas not under its sovereignty, and to constitute itself the repository of authority and the agent of destiny in regard thereto." The American Government also indicated that " the new situations must have been developed to a point warranting the removal of ' special ' safeguarding restrictions ".

Fifthly and lastly, the American Government was willing to discuss with the other countries concerned " any proposals based on justice and reason " for a revision of a treaty of which it is a party, " at whatever time and in whatever place may be commonly agreed upon ".

As summed up above, the second American note elucidates most candidly and in detail the traditional and present American policy towards Far Eastern problems as well as the nature and condition of the proposed new order as interpreted by the United States.   When one examines the note closely, however, one will not fail to discover a confusion of thought involved therein—a confusion for which the Japanese Government, too, is responsible, but because of which the American presentation is rendered less effective.   Namely, it is the error of taking the present conditions in China for what the new order would be like.   As a matter of fact, Japan is not claiming that all of the new situations created since the outbreak of hostilities should be the new order ; nor does she arbitrarily claim as legitimate whatever may be constructed in the name of the new order.   To have a new order accepted as legitimate would necessarily involve diplomatic negotiations and international readjustments.   Surely no treaty revision could be brought about arbitrarily.   Japan is only suggesting a need for revision.   In assuming that Japan intended arbitrary revision, the American Government committed a gross mistake. Foreign Minister Arita must have been partially responsible for this mistake, nevertheless, the United States Government misunderstood the policy of the Japanese Government. Only when Japan claims the existing conditions in China as a new order and, if and when Japan acts contrary to new international agreements reached after formal diplomatic negotiations on this question of the new order, will the American Government be able to employ rightfully and effectively most of the words which it used in its note of December 31, 1938.

There are indications, however, in this American note that the United States would in any case object to the new order, or would not agree to it even if it were achieved by just and reasonable processes.   But this is a question which is directly related to the Far Eastern policies of the two countries and must depend upon future developments..   So much can at least be said now, namely that there must be some tasks in China which should reasonably be recognized as specially Japan's in view of the special relations between the two countries. Anybody unwilling to recognize even such special situations, but persevering always in recognizing only the theoretical relations between country and country, would be unreasonably disregarding the actual circumstances of international relations behind the sanctity of treaties. In other parts of the world such special situations *do* exist, and they *are* recognized.

The Japanese Government has yet to discuss the matter fully with the American Government and make reasonable and effective counter-arguments. And undoubtedly such conversations will take place in due course.

The Anglo-Japanese Conversations and Anti-British Movement in Japan

Japan's foreign policy in 1939 was confusion itself. Confronted with the American note referred to above and with the British note of January 14, 1939, of a similar nature, the Japanese Government appeared to be quite in the dark. However, there were many reasons for this. First was the retirement of the Konoye Cabinet. Secondly, the Hiranuma Cabinet which succeeded was too much absorbed in the question of a Japan-Germany-Italy military alliance, which was an open secret at that time and was generally regarded as one of the causes of Prince Konoye's resignation. Thirdly, there were wanting new developments such as further consolidation of the plan for readjustment of Sino-Japanese relations, in order to reply clearly to the American and the British notes.

The farther the China Affair progressed and the more difficult its settlement became, the more fully Japan realized its international bearings. While seeking to settle the China Affair on a regional basis, *viz.*, a new order in East Asia,

Japan was at the same time falling more and more under the influence of the belief that, without taking sides in the world-wide struggle of totalitarianism versus democracy, settlement of the Affair would be impossible. This belief had a ready appeal to that national sentiment which could not but be roused by the pro-Chinese policy of Great Britain, and it resulted in strong pressure being exerted upon the governmental authorities.

Thus anti-British feeling sought every opportunity of demonstrating itself. It was not accidental that the question of the Tientsin, Kulangsu and Shanghai Concessions should have suddenly emerged as an important political issue, alongside the question of the Japan-Germay-Italy military alliance then under discussion in Tokyo. The scene at the Tientsin Concession, which was regarded as the base of the " pro-Chiang Kai-shek " activities of the British, looked especially unsatisfactory. In such circumstances, it was clearly impossible for the Japanese Government to negotiate with the British and the American Governments on the question of the new order ; for being of necessity general and legal, such negotiations on the question of the new order could not easily be made compatible with the negotiations over the concession issue, which were essentially specific and non-legal. And it was understandable that, while the former were left at a standstill, the latter should have been pushed vigorously by Japan as if in that way the difficulty in China might be solved, and that a nation-wide anti-British movement should have been organized in order to obtain British acquiescence. It should be remembered that the sentiments of the Japanese people are apt to be " mobilized " in such a direction. Further, in spite of the parallel policy of Great Britain and the United States, only.the former was made the object of attack while a most conciliatory attitude was shown towards the latter. This fact shows how strongly the European situation characterized by the Anglo-German rivalry appealed to the Japanese people.

A foreign policy for a new order in East Asia, however, is by no means a world policy to be hitched to the European policy of Germany or Italy. It should above all else be an East-Asiatic policy of Japan's own making and it should also be a policy seeking an understanding with Great Britain and the United States. For no matter how unpopular and objectionable such orientation may be to the Japanese people, Japan will unavoidably be confronted with the question of seeking this understanding, when faced with the persistent non-recognition policy of these two powers.

In point of this fact, soon after the breakdown of the Anglo-Japanese conversations over the Tientsin question, the conclusion of the Soviet-German Non-Aggression Pact shattered whatever hope there had remained of the proposed military alliance. It also directly caused the resignation of the Hiranuma Cabinet. Scarcely had the Abe Cabinet been formed before the European war broke out, and the new Cabinet declared that Japan would " keep out of the European war and concentrate upon settlement of the China Affair ". Throughout the most recent months under the Abe and the Yonai Cabinets, it was not difficult to see where the focal point of Japanese foreign policy lay.

CHAPTER XIV

THE NEW ORDER IN EAST ASIA AND ITS BEARING UPON WORLD PEACE

The Conception of a New Order in East Asia as a New International Organization

At present, anxieties and uncertainties prevail everywhere as to how the new order in East Asia will bring a readjustment in the relations between Japan, China and other powers having interests in China, how the recently established Nationalist Government of China under Wang Ching-wei will progress, and how it will adjust their relations with the Kuomintang Government, and finally how they will reach any understanding with the interested powers, especially Great Britain and the United States.

As described in the preceding chapters, this Japanese policy of a new order in East Asia has not been a policy suddenly or accidentally conceived, but has been nationally formulated after long and serious deliberation and with a view to settling not only the present conflict but rather the age-long instability of the Far East. For the first time since the " opening " of the country in the Meiji era, Japan now possesses a national policy really her own, Japan is truly " supported by her own feet ". The success or failure of the policy will not, of course, depend solely upon Japan's will, but it must equally be admitted that the Japan of today with such a policy of her own is vastly different from the Japan of yesterday which, without any such policy, was simply accommodating herself as best as she could to the general world trends.

In what way, then, does this policy bear upon peace in hte

world, and what international organization does it envisage ? What will be the formula or process by which it can be attained ? In regard to these questions, public opinion in Japan is yet to be formulated. At present the Government does not seem to be sufficiently experienced to give any ready answer ; nor have the people been given a strong enough intellectual incentive.

What follows is only a tentative conclusion which the author has reached after studying, as objectively as possible, the historical facts of the past as well as the internal and external situations prevailing today.

As an international organization, or in its bearing upon world peace, the new order in East Asia will have the following characteristics :

First, it is one form of regional international organization. The new relationship of mutual reliance which Japan is inviting China to build jointly is neither the ordinary treaty relationship between one sovereign power and another, nor a simple " planetary " organization like the League of Nations, comprehending all the countries of the world. Its geographical boundaries may be somewhat ambiguous, but it is an organization which covers only a region inhabited by the nations or races possessing given qualifications at a given time. The " East Asia " envisaged by Japan comprises, for the present at least, Japan, Manchoukuo and China. This is so, because there exist common to these three countries political, economic and cultural conditions and because any other contiguous regions lack some of them, though geographically there is no reason why they should be excluded.

Secondly, the new order in East Asia is an organization in which nationality, independence and freedom are to be respected in the fullest sense of the terms. That the conflict between Japan and China in recent years had been characterized by a clash between Japan's territorial and economic imperial-

ism and China's demand for national unity and independence
is clear. That the present armed strife, whatever its immediate
occasion, was fundamentally caused by this issue is also clear.

This strife might be settled temporarily if Japan either
forcefully assumed the position of a conqueror or were beaten
back. But Japan never either intended to conquer China or
believed that she could. On the other hand, it is inconceiva-
ble that China might be able by herself to beat back Japan.
If such is the case, clearly there will be no other way of bringing about a Far Eastern stability of any duration, except by
discovering some common basis for readjustment between
the demands of both countries. The new order in East Asia
is one attempt to do this and, in this attempt at least, it can
claim its *raison d'être*.

Thirdly, the new order in East Asia is a form of cooperation or co-existence of states which ensures international
intercourse and world peace. The relationship within the new
order is closer than the ordinary relationship between states,
but it is not an alliance inimical to international peace ; nor is
it such a bloc as would interfere with intercourse with the
outside world. In fact, to have safeguarding provisions in
this connection will be a necessary requisite for the new order
in East Asia. It has come to be recognized increasingly of
late that the international organization of the future should
consist of a few such regional organizations established for
regions where they are possible and desirable. For it would
then reconcile the conflicting forces of modern times, *viz.*,
nationalism which tends to contract, and industrialism which
seeks to expand, and thus promote a sound development of
international organization as a whole. It would also ensure
equitable distribution of economic forces. This is, in fact,
what Japan has in mind when she claims, as she often does,
that international justice should be realized in the Far East.

International justice as interpreted by the United States and other countries emphasizes the observance of treaty rights and obligations. If this justice can be called a "static" justice, that advocated by Japan, which attaches the greatest importance to equitable distribution of economic forces, may be called a " dynamic " justice. These two justices are by no means contradictory, the difference being only where the emphasis is laid, and it is one aim of the new order in East Asia to seek an adjustment of these two. Thus it is clear that this regional organization is not exclusive or monopolistic, but is wide open to international intercourse.

The Method of Realizing a New Order in East Asia

The new order in East Asia could not possibly be realized by any arbitrary method. It could be realized only by that of diplomatic negotiation and the common consent of all parties concerned. However, this is a most difficult method; indeed, it looks so difficult to some people in Japan that they think it would be futile to attempt it. In their opinion, the only method of realizing the new order is to make it a *fait accompli*. In other countries, too, especially in England and America, there are perhaps not a few people who expect Japanese success in such diplomatic negotiation. Leaving it to the historians of the future to judge, we are of the opinion that the proper and only method of realizing the new order will be that of diplomatic negotiation.

The first thing to remember in such negotiation is that all of the facts and arrangements which have been, and will be, brought about during the course of the present conflict are not necessarily to be facts and arrangements within the new order. It has been pointed out in the preceding chapter that there has been a confusion in this connection in the negotiations with Great Britain and the United States. The new order can be claimed to be as established only when the *de jure* recognition by all parties has been conferred. This will necessitate a revision of the actual situations created as well as of the existing treaties in the Far East and for this purpose international conferences will have to be convened. But, as a matter of policy, it will be advantageous for all parties concerned to let any two countries reach an agreement prior to any multilateral conferences.

Secondly, it is clear that the international principles pertaining to China, especially those of the Open Door and equal opportunity, will at a number of points conflict with the principles of the new order. But in this connection distinction must be drawn between the trading rights of other countries in China and their trading practices or processes. The new order in East Asia does not propose to disregard or impair in any way the trading rights of other countries in China, although it would result in restricting or modifying at some points the practices or processes of that trade. Evidently such restrictions or modifications of trading practices could not be regarded as a disregard or impairment of trading rights. There seems, however, to have been both a lack of understanding and a difference of opinion on this point between Japan and other countries. This should be remedied and, given the will to understand on the part of every party, it will not be difficult to close the gap now existing.

Thirdly, the new order in East Asia will not depend for its success solely upon its technical perfection or the benefits it confers upon this region. Above everything else, it will depend upon whether it will promote peace in the Pacific and the world at large. Therefore, as the United States has frequently pointed out, any agreement concerning the new order would necessarily involve readjustment of other matters directly or indirectly affected. Any revision of the Nine-Power Treaty

would thus involve a new understanding by all parties concerned of the general questions common to Pacific countries as
well as those questions affecting particular countries. It does
not necessarily follow, however, that the negotiations for these
purposes should be conducted either simultaneously or at the
same place. Each or some of them may be undertaken sepa-
rately or at different times. In view of her past experiences in
" conference diplomacy ", Japan will probably object to the
method of dealing with all questions at the same time and place.
However, she will not fail to realize that all of them are essentially interdependent and mutually conditional. And it will
not be at all impossible to discover a compromise between the
diplomatic process preferred by Japan and that desired by the
advocates of collective security.

BIBLIOGRAPHY

COLLECTIONS AND WORKS IN JAPANESE

Asahi Newspaper Co. *Chōki Kensetsu eno Michi* (Toward a Durable Reconstruction). 1938.

GUSHIMA, KENZABURŌ. *Sekai Seiji to Shina Jihen* (China Affair and World Politics). 1940.

HARA, KATSU. *Tōa Kaihōron Josetsu* (A Treatise on Emancipation of Asia). 1940.

International Association of Japan. *Remmei Dattai Kankei Shobunsho* (Papers Relating to the Withdrawal of Japan from the League of Nations). 1933.

ISHII, KIKUJIRŌ. *Gaikō Yoroku*. 1929. (The English translation by W. R. Langdon, "Diplomatic Commentaries." 1936.)

Japanese Government, Foreign Office. *Gaimushō Kōhyō Shū* (Collection of Official Documents and Releases). Vols. 1–19. 1922–40.

Japanese Government, Foreign Office, Information Bureau. *Manshū Jihen oyobi Shanghai Jiken Kankei Kōhyō Shū* (Official Documents Relating to the Manchurian Incident and the Shanghai Incident). 1934.

Japanese Government, Foreign Office, Information Bureau. *Shina Jihen Kankei Kōhyō Shū* (Official Documents Relating to the China Affair). Vols. 1–5. 1937–40.

Japanese Government, Foreign Office, Research Bureau. *Dai Nippon Gaikō Bunsho* (Diplomatic Documents of Japan). Vols. 1–9. 1936–41.

KASHIMA, MORINOSUKE. *Teikoku Gaikō no Kihon Seisaku* (Basic Policies of Japanese Diplomacy). 1938.

KIYOSAWA, WATARU. *Gaikō Shi* (Diplomatic History: "A Cultural History of Modern Japan" Series, Vol. 3). 1941.

MIYAZAKI, MASAYOSHI. *Tōa Remmei Ron* (The Idea of East Asia Federation). 1938.

ŌTA, UNOSUKE. *Shin Shina no Tanjō* (Birth of New China). 1937.

OZAKI, HOTSUMI. *Arashi ni tatsu Shina* (China Stands in Storm). 1937.

OZAKI, HOTSUMI. *Gendai Shina Hihan* (Analysis of Modern China). 1938.

RŌYAMA, MASAMICHI. *Nichiman Kankei no Kenkyū* (Studies on Relations between Japan and Manchuria). 1933.

RŌYAMA, MASAMICHI. *Sekai no Henkyoku to Nippon no Sekai Seisaku* (Japanese Policy in the Changing World). 1938.

RŌYAMA, MASAMICHI. *Seiji Shi* (Contemporary Political History : " A Cultural History of Modern Japan " Series, Vol. 2). 1940.

RŌYAMA, MASAMICHI. *Tōa to Sekai* (East Asia and the World). 1941.

Shōwa Research Society. *Tōa Shinchitsujo Kensetsu no Riron to Hōhō* (Theory and Method for the Construction of New Order in East Asia). 1940.

SUGIHARA, MASAMI. *Tōa Kyōdōtai no Genri* (Principles of East Asia Confederacy). 1939.

TANAKA, KANAYE. *Tōa no Kaiten* (Evolution of East Asia). 1939.

TANAKA, NAOKICHI. *Sekai Seikyoku to Tōa Shinchitsujo* (World Politics and New Order in East Asia). 1939.

Tokyo Institute of Political and Economic Research. *Seiji Keizai Nenkan* (Political and Economic Annals of 1920–30). 1930.

Tokyo Institute of Political and Economic Research. *Sekai to' Nippon* (Japan and the World). 1934.

WATANABE, IKUJIRŌ. *Nippon Kinsei Gaikō Shi* (Modern Diplomatic History of Japan). 1938.

WATANABE, IKUJIRŌ. *Ippan Shi* (A General History : " A Cultural History of Modern Japan " Series, Vol. 1). 1941.

YABE, SADAJI. *Saikin Nippon Gaikō Shi* (Japanese Foreign Policy since the Restoration). 1940.

WORKS IN WESTERN LANGUAGES

AKAGI, R.H. Japan's Foreign Relations: 1542–1936. Tokyo. 1936.

BISSON, T.A. Japan in China. New York. 1938.

BISSON, T.A. American Policy in the Far East: 1931–1940. New York. 1940.

DULLES, FOSTER RHEA. Forty Years of American-Japanese Relations. New York & London. 1937.

FAHS, CHARLES B. Government in Japan. New York. 1940.

FRIEDMAN, IRVING S. British Relations with China: 1931–1939. New York. 1940.

GRISWOLD, A. WHITNEY. The Far Eastern Policy of the United States. New York. 1938.

HSÜ, SHUHSI. China and her Political Entity. New York. 1926.

HSÜ, SHUHSI. The North China Problem. Shanghai. 1937.

HUDSON, G.F. The Far East in World Politics. New York. 1937.

Institute of Pacific Relations. Problems of the Pacific, 1925, '27, '29, '31, '33, '36, '39. New York.

Kiel Universität. Weltwirtschaftliches Archiv. 46. Band, Heft I. Kiel. Juli 1937.

LATTIMORE, OWEN. Manchuria, Cradle of Conflict. New York. 1932.

LATTIMORE, OWEN. Inner Asian Frontiers of China. New York & London. 1940.

NITOBE, INAZŌ. Japan—Some Phases of her Problems and Development. London. 1931.

NITOBE AND OTHERS. Western Influences in Modern Japan. Chicago. 1931.

OKAKURA, KAKUZŌ. The Awakening of Japan. New York. 1921.

PEFFER, NATHANIEL. Prerequisites to Peace in the Far East. New York. 1940.

REISCHAUER, ROBERT KARL. Japan : Government—Politics. New York. 1939.

Royal Institute of International Affairs. China and Japan. London. 1938.

Royal Institute of International Affairs. British Far Eastern Policy. London. 1939.

SCHUMPETER, ALLEN, GORDON AND PENROSE. Industrialization in Japan and Manchoukuo : 1930–1940. New York. 1940.

SIMONDS, FRANK H. & EMENY, BROOKS. Great Powers in World Politics. New York. 1937.

TAKEUCHI, TATSUJI. War and Diplomacy in the Japanese Empire. New York. 1935.

Tokyo Gazette. (A Monthly Report of Current Politics, Official Statements and Statistics.)

WILLOUGHBY, WESTEL W. Japan's Case Examined. Baltimore. 1940.

YOUNG, CARL WALTER. The International Relations of Manchuria. Chicago. 1929.

YOUNG, CARL WALTER. Japan's Special Position in Manchuria. Baltimore. 1931.

YOUNG, CARL WALTER. The International Legal Status of the Kwantung Leased Territory. Baltimore. 1931.

YOUNG, CARL WALTER. Japanese Jurisdiction in the South Manchurian Railway Areas. Baltimore. 1931.

INDEX